✔ KT-217-018

ASPECTS OF MODERN SOCIOLOGY

General Editors

John Barron Mays   Professor of Sociology, University of Liverpool
Maurice Craft   Professor of Education, University of Nottingham

This Longman library of texts in modern sociology consists of three Series, and includes the following titles:

THE SOCIAL STRUCTURE OF MODERN BRITAIN

The family
Mary Farmer
University of Liverpool

The political structure
Grace Jones
King Alfred's College,
Winchester

Population
Prof. R. K. Kelsall
University of Sheffield

Education
Ronald King
University of Exeter

The welfare state
Prof. David Marsh
University of Nottingham

Crime and its treatment
Prof. John Barron Mays
University of Liverpool

Patterns of urban life
Prof. R. E. Pahl
University of Kent

The working class
Kenneth Roberts
University of Liverpool

The middle class
John Raynor
The Open University

Leisure
Kenneth Roberts
University of Liverpool

Adolescence
Cyril Smith
Social Science Research Council

The mass media
Peter Golding
University of Leicester

The legal structure
Michael Freeman
University of London

Rural life
Gwyn Jones
University of Reading

Religious institutions
Joan Brothers
University of London

Mental illness
Bernard Ineichen
University of Bristol

Forthcoming titles will include:

Minority groups
Eric Butterworth
University of York

The economic structure
Prof. Cedric Sandford
University of Bath

Aspects of modern sociology

SOCIAL RESEARCH

GENERAL EDITORS

John Barron Mays
Eleanor Rathbone Professor of Sociology,
University of Liverpool

Maurice Craft
Professor of Education
University of Nottingham

006355

THE HENLEY COLLEGE LIBRARY

SOCIAL PROCESSES

Bureaucracy
Dennis Warwick
University of Leeds

Social control
C. Ken Watkins
University of Leeds

Communication
Prof. Denis McQuail
University of Amsterdam

Stratification
Prof. R. K. Kelsall
University of Sheffield
and
H. Kelsall

Industrialism
Barry Turner
University of Exeter

Social change
Anthony Smith
University of Reading

Socialisation
Graham White
University of Liverpool

Forthcoming titles will include:

Social conflict
Prof. John Rex
University of Warwick

Migration
Prof. J. A. Jackson
University of Dublin

SOCIAL RESEARCH

The limitations of social research
Prof. M. D. Shipman
University of Warwick

Social research design
Prof. E. Krousz
University of Newcastle
and
S. H. Miller
City University

Sources of official data
Kathleen Pickett
University of Liverpool

History of social research methods
Gary Easthope
University of East Anglia

Deciphering data
Jonathan Silvey
University of Nottingham

The philosophy of social research
John Hughes
University of Lancaster

Forthcoming titles will include:

Data collection in context
Stephen Ackroyd
and
John Hughes
University of Lancaster

160049

BY THE SAME AUTHOR
The sociology of the school (1968)
Education and modernisation (1971)
Staff-student relations (1971)
Childhood, a sociological perspective (1972)
Inside a curriculum project (1974)
Curriculum: an introduction (1976) with D. Jenkins
The organisation and impact of social research (1976) editor
In-school evaluation (1978)

The limitations of social research

MARTEN SHIPMAN B.SC. (SOC), PH.D.
Professor of Education
University of Warwick

Second Edition

SOUTH OXFORDSHIRE
TECHNICAL COLLEGE
LIBRARY
Henley-on-Thames

Longman London and New York

Longman Group Limited
Longman House
Burnt Mill, Harlow, Essex, UK

Published in the United States of America
by Longman Inc., New York

© Longman Group Limited 1973, 1981

All rights reserved. No part of this publication may be
reproduced, stored in a retrieval system, or transmitted in any
form or by any means, electronic, mechanical, photocopying,
recording, or otherwise, without the prior permission of the
Copyright owner.

First published 1973

Second edition 1981

British Library Cataloguing in Publication Data
Shipman, Marten Dorrington
  Limitations of social research. — 2nd ed.
  1. Social science research.
  I. Title
  300′.7′2   H62   80-40764
  ISBN 0-582-29526-2

Printed in Singapore by
Kua Co., Book Manufacturer, Pte Ltd

CONTENTS

EDITORS' PREFACE

The first series in Longman's *Aspects of Modern Sociology* library was concerned with the social structure of modern Britain, and was intended for students following professional and other courses in universities, polytechnics, colleges of education, and elsewhere in further and higher education, as well as for those members of a wider public wishing to pursue an interest in the nature and structure of British society.

This further series sets out to examine the history, aims, techniques and limitations of social research, and it is hoped that it will be of interest to the same readership. It will seek to offer an informative but not uncritical introduction to some of the methodologies of social science.

John Barron Mays
Maurice Craft

FOREWORD

This second edition takes account of the profound changes that have taken place in the social sciences, and particularly in Sociology, across the last decade. These changes have confirmed the need for informed scepticism, for a recognition of both the limitations of social research, and of its scope. The purpose of the book remains, therefore, to provide a guide for the majority, not on how to design social investigations, but on how to assess the credibility of research already published. It is addressed first to students of social science, second to those, particularly in education, who use the evidence from social research, and third, to the public who meet such evidence through the mass media.

Just as the normal book on research methods gives an incomplete picture of the actual research process, so the extent of the changes in social research methods are often slow to percolate through the public. The image remains the social survey, even though this has been under particularly heavy fire. Similarly, the increased emphasis on research that accepts the authenticity of spontaneous accounts rather than the responses to questions contrived by the researcher, is often not appreciated. The strengths and weaknesses of different methods are not made apparent in books on research methods, and public appreciation of changing approaches to social research lags behind practice.

Another reason for revision was that many of the controversies used to illustrate the difficulties in reaching agreement over the implications of evidence have deepened into fierce political battles within education. Other controversies have been added to demonstrate how new methods produce fresh problems in interpretation. The revised edition has involved therefore, not only updating, but fuller consideration of the changing theoretical positions that lie beneath the often very different approaches to social research.

For the consumer of social research there are three key questions. They should be asked about evidence, whether the source of doubt lies in the political beliefs of the researcher, the conceptual framework in which he has worked, the design chosen, or the techniques used in data collection, analysis, interpretation and publication. Indeed, whenever evidence is to be used these questions should be asked, just as they should be about this book.

Key Question 1

If the investigation had been carried out by someone other than the author, using his methods, would the same results have been obtained? The concern here is with the reliability of the methods used. This includes a consideration of the methods used for gathering information and the dependability of the researcher. Approaches such as observation, questionnaires and interviews used in the social sciences are never completely reliable and there are always opportunities for distortion through the influence of the investigator and his interaction with the subjects of the study.

Key Question 2

Does the evidence really reflect the reality under examination? The concern here is with validity. Different researchers might obtain similar evidence by using similar methods, but this reliability might conceal a failure to really survey, measure, indicate or observe the phenomenon under consideration. Consistent results may not get near the truth. The chances of such failure are increased by the interaction between the researcher and his subjects, the imposition of his definitions on theirs, their ability to interpret and adjust to his motives and their skill in managing their responses. The picture presented may be consistent, but may still be unrelated to reality. Human actions, attributes and attitudes are subtle. Research methods are crude. The evidence presented may not be valid, and this may be concealed by the apparent complexity of the analysis presented.

Key Question 3

What relevance do the results have beyond the actual research?
The concern here is with the extent to which results can be generalised. Samples may be unrepresentative. Individuals under observation tend not to behave naturally. Results from research in any one place or at any one time may not be applicable in others. Human individuals and human groups are marked by their variety. Generalisation from one to another may be misleading.

Key Question 4

Is there sufficient detail on the way the evidence was produced for the credibility of the research to be assessed?
This book contains controversies as introductions to each chapter. Each of these is on an important educational issue. To decide between the often conflicting evidence presented by researchers, the consumer must be able to assess the work using the three key questions above. The responsibility of the researcher is to ensure that sufficient information is presented to allow the reader to do this.

This responsibility of the researcher to provide his audience with detail of his research procedures applies regardless of the research approach used. When the approach is based on the methods of the natural sciences via surveys or experiment, it is conventional to include a passage on the procedures, although this is often too streamlined to be a basis for assessing credibility. When the approach is phenomenological, trying to show how people make sense of their social relationships, there is no possibility of following a Hypothesis, Methods, Results, Conclusions format. Indeed, it is the rejection of the determinism in this natural science model that is the unifying force in much recent social science. But the responsibility to give the reader a clear picture of the way accounts were collected remains. Indeed, while the first three key questions are essentially derived from, and applicable to, methods derived from the natural sciences, they have to be asked of all research by those who will use it. For social scientists, for teachers, administrators, politicians, parents and public, the weight that can be put on social science as a basis for action has to be assessed, not only to decide amongst the contrasting evidence from the various subjects, but between this evidence and journalism covering the same important topics. The distinguishing feature of scientific reporting is that methods are made public. That obligation applies to everyone working with the title of behavioural, human and social, as well as natural, scientist.

DO TEACHING STYLES AFFECT PUPIL PROGRESS?

In April 1976, Neville Bennett and his fellow researchers in the University of Lancaster published *Teaching Styles and Pupil Progress*.[1] Few books have received such media coverage. It hit the national press overnight. *The Times Educational Supplement* distributed copies to reviewers in advance so that in the issue on the Friday following publication there were central page spreads of summary, comment and criticism.[2] In each of the major journals there were extended reviews and articles. The authors counter-punched their critics with vigour. There were television and radio broadcasts, questions in the House of Commons and in education committees.

The furore can only be understood by the timing of the book. 1976 was a critical year for education. It was the year of the William Tyndale school enquiry, the House of Commons Expenditure Committee's report on the attainments of the school-leaver, the Yellow Book prepared by the D.E.S. and the Prime Minister's speech at Ruskin College. All these events were symptomatic of what has since been described as the start of *Schooling in Decline*.[3] Significantly it was also the year when expenditure on education stopped growing and when falling rolls hit the intakes to secondary schools in city areas. The Lancaster research on primary schooling was dropped into this debate with aplomb by a new publishing firm. That 10,000 copies were sold on the first day was not surprising.[4] Neither was it surprising that this turned out to be the classic educational controversy over research findings. The academics slugged it out to the joy of editors. Some concentrated on the study itself. But much wider issues were raised. Thus from one corner Miller applauded Bennett for researching into something of practical importance, and attacked critics for their lack of action and surfeit of theorising.[5] In the other corner McIntyre pressed for researchers to report only to people who were technically competent to evaluate their work.[6] Bennett's short-comings were not seen as confined to technical incompetence, but to trying to communicate with teachers about matters that were beyond them.

The *Times Educational Supplement* of 30 April 1976 ran three pages of reviews.[7] These were neatly balanced, one hostile from two American researchers, one uncritical from a headmaster and one guarded by a researcher. But it also included comments from Rhodes Boyson and the Confederation for the Advancement of State Education.[8] The former saw the work as breaking the conspiracy of silence surrounding progressive primary schooling, while the latter were surprised that parental influence was not considered. These appeared with brief comments from Bennett under the headline 'Dr Bennett shrugs off Black Paper Connec-tion'. Gray, later to emerge as leading hatchet man, also reported that his own research had produced different results. On 7 May the *T.E.S.* gave a background report on the publishers of the book and Gray gave more details of his own research.[9] Sinha added a letter, pointing out that his college of education had produced two of the research team including Bennett, that they were indeed child-centred in their views, but that this did not indicate indoctrination by himself or fellow tutors.[10] On the 14 May, Clegg returned to England and wrote to ask what the fuss was about.[11] De Bono also took the opportunity to link Bennett's evidence to his own interest in the teaching of thinking.[12] On the 21 May, Bennett and Entwistle replied to their critics.[13] This was a technical counter-attack, but also accused the critics of innuendo and inaccuracy. Predictably, on the 28 May Walker published a letter under the heading 'Such a silly debate',[14] and Hughes another under 'It's just common sense'.[15] The *T.E.S.* wound up the debate on 4 June. There was a three-page centre-spread from Bennett, Bruner, Entwistle, Marsh, Owen and Rogers.[16] Gray also wrote that his contribution three issues before had been misunderstood in Bennett and Entwistle's response a fortnight later because the *T.E.S.* had left out part of his evidence.[17] Unfortunately this had made it seem that his evidence supported rather than opposed that of Bennett. Fortunately the *T.E.S. Scotland* had published the full text, giving the Celts the chance to see what the Sassenachs had missed.

A similar series of reviews and letters appeared in *New Society*. Here however, Bennett was more fortunate for Bruner wrote a very favourable review.[18] He was indeed enthusiastic enough to have also written the introduction to the American version of the book. The major technical criticism in *New Society* came from Satterly.[19] All the major educational journals later carried extended reviews. The most enjoyable were in *Educational Research*. Here Gray and Satterly joined forces to contribute 'A Chapter of errors: Teaching Styles and Pupil Progress in Retrospect'[20] which stated: 'Given a research design that is so flawed it is doubtful whether any meaningful conclusions can be drawn from the study.' Bennett and Entwistle soon followed with 'Rite and Wrong: A Reply to "A chapter of errors".'[21] Neatly they suggested that Gray and Satterly had written prematurely in the heat of the popular furore, as well as being wrong, performing a rite and mis-stating the conclusions of the book. The knockabout fun was in danger of obscuring the importance of the debate.

As usual in these controversies, the reviews became balanced once the temperature cooled. *The Harvard Educational Review* of 1977 not only carried two lengthy articles, but the Atlantic divide enabled these reviewers to point to two factors; selection at 11 years and the strong influence of parental occupation on attainment in Britain that should not have been ignored.[22] But by this time the evaluations of Follow Through, the successor of the Head Start programmes, were partially supporting Bennett's conclusions about the benefits of formal styles and his evidence could be put into a wider context.

There is no point in reproducing the technical dispute over *Teaching Styles and Pupil Progress*. They are well documented and the data is still being reanalysed. But one aspect is important. Much of the criticism revolved around technical points which probably made little difference. But there were less technical design decisions that could have been very influential. The most obvious was the way the teachers were categorised into formal, informal or mixed styles. Twelve categories were identified, not by observing teachers in action, but by their perception of their own style. Of these 12 categories 1 and 2 were grouped as 'informal', 3, 4 and 7 as 'mixed' and 11 and 12 as 'formal'. Now there is clearly a problem in collapsing categories in this way. Many factors which could make up the package that defines degree of formality were ignored. The teachers could have practised very different styles to those they professed. They probably varied their styles between classes, groups and individual children. The 'mixed' category does seem a rag-bag. The important point is that there were only 12 teachers in each of the three 'styles' and small errors in allocation could have had large effects on the results. There was also a sampling problem among the pupils. There may have been some 400 per teaching style, but results for types of pupil are reported for as few as 4 pupils in one type, and discussions of high and low achievers in different types of classroom sometimes refer to less than 10 children.

This criticism of Bennett has to be placed in the context of the task he set himself. It was important to produce evidence to supplement that already in existence. All attempts to find what is involved in effective teaching have failed so far. No research has identified the features in teachers that can raise pupil attainment. It is doubtful whether any prediction from teaching style to pupil progress would pay off. There are so many factors inside and outside the school that we even have to debate whether schools have any effect. The choice may be to go on trying, with the risk of producing frail evidence, or to contract educational research to private communication between academics. My own view is that research evidence is one kind among many. It is the responsibility of researchers to produce it, to secure the maximum reliability and validity, publish it, but not to claim superiority over evidence collected by teachers, advisors, inspectors and so on. It is different, not superior, in the criteria used for validation. Its claim to respect is that the methods used are not only tried and possible to replicate, but that they are published for others to answer the key questions which introduced this book. In this sense the controversy over Bennett's research was part of the way evidence should be assessed for credibility.

1

SCIENTIFIC ACTIVITY IN THEORY AND PRACTICE

This book is a consumer's guide to social research. Such guidance is necessary because scientists tend to manage the impression that they give to the public. This management combines both mystery and discipline. The mystery enables scientists to exclude the bogus, but also the public, from influence over their work. This can be sustained by private languages, academic journals and distinctive qualifications. The discipline is exercised by established members of the scientific community qualifying students, refereeing appointments and publications and approving the standing of evidence.

Many social scientists reject this exclusiveness. But without the claim to be scientific, no boundary can be drawn that excludes the journalist, the novelist or even the crank. Without the claim, the prestige and resources will not be forthcoming. Furthermore, that the bid for scarce resources provided by the public has to be based on their definition of science. However much social scientists object to being categorised as using the methods of the natural sciences, that is usually the basis of their claim when viewed by those who provide the money for research. Hence research is often dressed-up before publication and hence the need for a definition of limitations, and a look behind the public face to see the private practice.

The window-dressing can be seen in the layout of the scientific paper. Medawar has argued that such papers are frauds because they suggest that the observations made in the experiment impinged on an open mind.[1] Only then is there a discussion of the meaning of the results obtained. In reality all scientific enquiry starts with expectations about the outcome. The scientist selects his problem, designs his research and analyses his results by reference to existing theory. The key stage in research, the formulation of hypotheses, consists of hunches derived in this way. Science is normally problem solving, not a thrust into the unknown.

Medawar is drawing a distinction between two parts of scientific research. There is the inspiration, creation, imagination and guesswork that finally leads to a hypothesis. There is then deduction from this hunch, followed by a second stage that can be a rigorous process of testing of the ideas. Both come from within the same discipline. But the real sequence of scientific research is inspiration then observation, not observation then inspiration as implied in streamlined written papers. Normal science consists of problem solving with the results anticipated because they will fit into the existing jigsaw. The imaginative stage occurs as the problem is first defined. As the data is collected it impinges on a mind already anticipating it. The scientific paper reverses the real sequence in order to preserve the impression of science as an inductive activity.

This convention for reporting science is part of the mystery that obscures the actual organisation of science from the public. It is not only that scientific communities develop private conventions for reporting research, private languages, professional associations and professional journals, but that within each community there are few at the centre of communications, prestige and power and many on the periphery. The producers of evidence tend to be central where the funds for research are available. On the fringes of the community are the wholesalers, including the teachers, using this evidence, often in subjects centred outside and with a restricted view of actual production. Finally there are the consumers, whether students hoping to gain entry or the lay public, who have to take reliability and validity on trust. In doing so they are taught to accept the conventions. Only the few students who take higher degrees, find a sponsor for research and are accepted into the academic life at the centre get to see the reality behind the presented picture.

The existence of a large peripheral group on the fringe of a small scientific community is particularly worrying in education where there are around half a million teachers and support staff forming an audience for research. In this large group who retail information are a smaller group of wholesalers in teacher education, in-service and advisory work. Finally there is a small group, largely within the universities and polytechnics, who actually produce the evidence. The consequences of this pyramid of influence have been unfortunate. First, the disputes within the scientific communities of economics, psychology, sociology and so on are fought within academia. Their intensity is often not appreciated from the outside. Second, the changes that result from these disputes percolate only slowly into the world where evidence is used. Third, and most important, evidence is produced for colleagues, for editors, for referees and to influence internal disputes which are largely invisible to the wholesalers and retailers. The result is that evidence is often accepted uncritically. The nightmares associated with intelligence testing, with theories of cultural deprivation and with teaching that assumes discrete linguistic codes arose because the scepticism among the research community was not appreciated by teachers, their advisers or by policy-makers. Evidence is viewed less critically as the distance from the producers increases.

The existence of a large army of potential users is rarely considered by those who research or write using evidence from research. The language used is usually exclusive. It is the language of journals, of seminars, of symposia and conferences. It is not written in the language of those who teach in school, advise, inspect or make policy. This situation is exacerbated by the speed of social change that makes evidence redundant and by the speed at which social science advances. The joy of research here is that each piece of evidence, however modest, is new and may be influential. The higher degree thesis is still likely to be a breakthrough.

The situation for the consumers of evidence is also exacerbated by the way books on research methods are usually written. They suggest mechanistic, routine procedures, often confined to survey research. In practice, routine procedures even where followed, are often interrupted by flashes of insight that change the direction of the work, or lead to short-cutting. It is rare to progress smoothly through a predetermined sequence even in uncomplicated research. Ingenuity and tenacity are usually needed for completion. Furthermore, the technical stage, where predetermined techniques may be used, is preceded by a creative stage and followed by another. Decisions about techniques follow decisions about the way the problem being investigated is related to theoretical ideas and existing evidence. Once data has been collected, analysis and generalisation once again require theorising.

Scientists at work

It is misleading to suggest that scientists always work in conventional ways, or finish with facts that are irrefutable. The actual process of research may follow no logical pattern. This reality is often concealed from the public. Scientists make their work public in a way that omits false starts, dead ends and changes in direction. Natural scientists and, increasingly, social scientists are members of communities and avoid exposing their criticisms of each other, however vicious these are in private. Communities within the social sciences may be less cohesive but the impression is still given to outsiders that members research according to established rules.

In this book the concern is with recognised, respectable and publicised research. Below this, students and enthusiastic amateurs are active in practising the necessary techniques. Some consequences of this can be gauged in a study of ninety-eight anthropology students in California who were set an exercise in collecting information on a topic of their choice.[2] The consequences were described in an article titled 'Unleashing the untrained'. The author and organiser described the effect as 'methodological and ethical violence'. The choices ranged from examining the body beautiful to participant observation of drinking bouts. The students investigated relentlessly with a blatant disregard for the rights of others. They gave away confidences, acted as Peeping Toms, reported illegal practices, violated promised anonymity and obtained information by fraud. They obtained and used tests that required long training for proper administration. One stirred up an industrial dispute. The author cheerfully concluded that his students had done irreparable damage to the chances of those who might follow in the search for information. There is truly a Gresham's Law of research. The bad drives out the good.

The assessment of evidence in the social sciences depends on visualising the reality behind the written account of research. The reader should be an iconoclast, smashing the image of research as a methodical, consistent process following agreed rules of procedure. Visualise as a stimulus to such a sceptical attitude the work of McCaghy and Skipper published under the titles 'Lesbian behaviour as an adaptation to the occupation of stripping' and 'Stripteasers: the anatomy and career contingencies of a deviant occupation'.[3] These two professors of sociology report that their observations and interviews took place in clubs and burlesque theatres in ten large cities located between Honolulu and New York, New Orleans and Chicago. Having watched the performance they were introduced to the girls backstage as professors doing an anthology on burlesque. Diligently making sure that they were both present they interviewed thirty-five strippers on the spot, or in a nearby bar or restaurant. The written account must have been dull compared with the actual fieldwork. Behind the table comparing the height, waist, bust and hip measurements of the sample, compared with Playboy Playmates of the month and the average American women may lie research activity rarely associated with scientists.

There are few studies of scientists at work.[4] Those there are give a very human picture of frustrations and joy, inspiration and depression, false starts and premature finishes. An example is Coleman's account of the progress of his work on 'The adolescent society'.[5] The start was a conversation between Coleman and Trow and their wives. Each had experienced a different type of schooling. This interested Coleman in the way prestige was allocated in high schools by the officials and by the adolescents. The first research proposals were written in 1954. Involvement in other work and a failure to obtain funds delayed the start until 1957.

Coleman's interest in the allocation of prestige was allied to his involvement in developing new methods of collecting data on social systems rather than individuals. However, when the analysis of data was started in 1958, it could not be used for its intended purpose. Coleman then changed the focus of the study from social system to role. Both the hypotheses and the methods of analysis were altered. The work was written in 1959, the manuscript was ready in 1960 and was published in 1961. In the seven years the work had changed, not only as a result of financial difficulties but because the data did not live up to its promise.

Similar experiences were reported by Thomas and Znaniecki at a conference in 1938 arranged to discuss their book, *The Polish Peasant in Europe and America*, published twenty years before.[6] Thomas wanted to study immigrant problems, an important issue in North America in the early part of this century, and in 1908 received financial backing. He had the money and the hunch but no materials. His search for documentary evidence on Polish life involved adventures connected with the outbreak of the First World War that were not only unanticipated, but resulted in much material being left in a central European hotel by a courier fleeing from the authorities to avoid being called up for the army. Again none of this farce appeared in the final books where the actual method of collecting the data was largely ignored. Indeed, Thomas admitted twenty years afterwards that the notes on methods in Volume 1 of the book were not based on the actual methods used, but were theoretical ideas developed by him as a lecturer. The conference organised by the Social Science Research Council in which the authors discussed their book and a critical commentary on it with other social scientists is unique. It is unlikely that many books would stand up as well to such examination, yet the impression remains of a published version that glossed over many shortcomings and included much that gave a false impression of meticulous scientific method. Similarly the generalisations made stretched far beyond those actually derived from the data. Finally, the retrospective comments by the two authors confirmed the common feeling of dissatisfaction with a work once it is in print.

These confusions and frustrations rarely appear in print. Books and articles consist of selections of successful investigations, pruned of those parts of the total work that did not lead to confirmation of a hypothesis. This convention probably does little harm within a profession that can interpret the written version, but by the time the article has been popularised in book form, any suggestions of irregularity are eliminated and the lay reader is given an impression of order that is very removed from actual practice.

The third exercise is to relate the popular versions of the research back to the original. Education is particularly open to the results of popularisation because it has to draw its information from a number of academic disciplines. The educationalist is outside the discipline in which the original work with which he is concerned was done. Consequently it is difficult to appreciate the specific difficulties that may have been met in the original research. An official report such as *Children and their Primary Schools*[7] has to blend actual practice in schools with developments in social science. Thus a chapter on children learning in school presents evidence from researchers such as Pavlov and Skinner, Isaacs and Piaget, and uses this to make statements about the value of play, discovery and activity. The work of social scientists are selected and then used to recommend some practices and discourage others, but without any discussion of the many criticisms of the selected work, or of the existence of alternative theories that could suggest different practices. Indeed, the social sciences are frequently used to justify existing fashion rather than as an objective basis for reform.

The incidental happenings in research are also pruned in writing up and only those steps which lead directly to proof or disproof of the hypothesis appear in the written report. The reasons for this retrospective falsification of changes of hypothesis, alterations in research design and the interference by uncontrolled peripheral influences lie primarily in the professional codes established in each academic discipline. In the social sciences particularly, the need to establish a position among the sciences necessitates a formality in reporting research that is often out of touch with the actual reliability of the procedures.

In practice chance occurrences during research have often proved more important than the original subject. Pasteur recognised that attenuated pathogens could be used for immunisation against disease as a result of trying to revive cultures which he had left while on vacation.[8] The most famous recent case has been Fleming's observations on the inhibition of bacterial growth by a mould which led to the development of penicillin. In all these cases it is the knowledge of the scientist which alerts him to the importance of the chance development. The term 'serendipity' was coined in the eighteenth century to describe this facility of researchers to exploit the chance discovery such as the *penicillium notatum* mould.

The existence of researchers willing to wander away from their mainstream of interest to pursue chance developments indicates a basic division among scientists. Some maintain that science should be imaginative and creative, while others support a science that follows clearly defined rules of procedure without deviation. The crucial perspective for the non-specialist is of science as an area of controversy and of scientists as fallible, argumentative, ambitious human beings like the rest of us, but constrained within often tight-knit communities. The examples from sociological research and from disputes over psychological and historical research cited later show the depth of this disagreement which is often concealed to the reader of books.

The way scientists actually work, and the impact of everyday matters upon their work can be gauged from the following case of the floppy-eared rabbits.[9] Two comparable medical scientists both noticed that rabbits injected with papain suffered from an amusing collapsing of the ears. Neither could devote much time to the phenomenon which did not seem to have any practical significance. However, one did try to obtain a rapid explanation of the ear collapse. He used his knowledge to do the expected tests. In reality these tests were selective, based on his ideas of what was likely to be the cause, the usual, but not the textbook procedure. He ignored the effect on cartilage because he had learned that this was not considered interesting. The other doctor too was amused, but used the ear collapse as a test of the potency of papain rather than trying to find a cause of the collapsing ears. Other work concerned with muscles also led him away from considering cartilage as the crucial area and also took up all his energy. The first doctor later chanced to show his students the collapse of the rabbit's ears and because he was in front of students he carried out the correct procedures rather than short-cutting according to his accumulated knowledge as he had done before and which was his, and other scientists', usual practice. Because he had more time at this moment, because he was getting students used to experimental pathology, and because there happened to be a large supply of rabbits available, he could carry out a systematic, controlled examination. By comparing injected and normal rabbits and taking sections from the ears of both he detected the change in the cartilage that provided the explanation.

These examples of serendipity lost and serendipity gained

illustrate the way scientists use their knowledge of experimental variables to short-circuit textbook research procedures. In this case the knowledge of both doctors stopped them from looking at the cartilage which they considered unimportant and in which, because of the emphasis of their major research interests, they were not interested. Only when a teaching situation forced one to carry out formal comparisons between injected and normal rabbits was the rather obvious difference in cartilage revealed, much to the shame of the doctors concerned. Usually the short-circuiting is harmless. Scientific inquiry is rarely inductive, but always influenced by the preconceptions of the researcher which enable him to select among his data and concentrate on the important parts.

What is distinctive about science

What then distinguishes scientific research from investigation by journalists or novelists? First, it is the degree of control exercised over the research. Second, it is the way that control is opened to public scrutiny. If a social scientist follows an interest by observing what strikes his eye, recording the memorable and writing what seems interesting, there is no claim to be scientific, however valuable the observations may be when guided by the insights of sociology or some other social science. There has to be some measure of control over the selection, definition, observation of the phenomenon concerned and some concern over reliability and validity. The 'how to do it' research manual is useful in providing controlled methods, but the same principle applies where the protection of the natural situation is a first priority. There has also to be control over the context in which the observations, questioning or measurements are made. Crowd behaviour at Milwall F.C. observed when the home team is winning differs from when they are losing, and you get different results from questioning school leavers in the deputy head's study than in youth clubs.

The final and most controversial area of control is over the subjects themselves. Here the danger of trivialising is great. Any control may distort. To obtain validity it may be necessary to observe without the subjects knowing that they are being scrutinised. In such cases the only control exercised is over the researcher and the way the observations are made. But asking questions, and observing as an identifiable outsider, are obtrusive and will influence the subjects of the research.

There is therefore a spectrum of research methods stretching from the rigidly controlled laboratory experiment to loosely controlled observation in a natural situation. But this spectrum of available approaches to research is not just a menu from which researchers pick according to the phenomenon they are investigating. A psychologist carrying out a laboratory experiment with humans is likely to be exercising control to approximate to the methods used in the natural sciences. Such methods have been successful in the study of natural phenomena, and if the object is to establish a social science that can predict human behaviour from present circumstances it has seemed profitable to adopt natural scientific conventions.

This view of science as a search for laws confirmed through empirical methods such as observation, survey and experiment raises questions about the way evidence is to be confirmed or rejected. These are epistemological questions about the criteria for establishing knowledge as valid. Mystical, non-observable revelations tend to be rejected and the scientist checks statements of fact, laws and theories against observable data. Confirmation should come from observations and tests from scientists, regardless of their theoretical, political or religious positions. It is seen as a value-neutral and objective way of checking validity.

This positivist view of science has been challenged from within the natural, as well as in the social, sciences. Fundamental to the alternative position to the traditional, positivist view of science as law-seeking is the conviction that laws and relations between phenomena do not explain that phenomena. Thus laws of motion relating to falling bodies can be established through observation and measurement, but an explanation of the phenomenon of free fall requires some concept such as gravity that can not be derived through observation or experiment. Similarly, in the social sciences it may be possible to show empirically that humans get aggressive when frustrated. But this doesn't explain why people respond to being baulked by getting aggressive. Understanding requires some interpretation of the meanings attached to such behaviour by those frustrated. In this interpretation the main criteria of validity are not objectivity in observations, but consistency in interpretation. Imagination and intuition are accepted as part of the process through which scientists try to understand phenomena.

This debate between those who hold a traditional law-seeking, hypothesis-testing view of science, and those who stress understanding through interpretation and imagination recurs throughout this book. Frequently, apparently objective fact is shown to be essentially subjective. The safest stance for the reader is to remain sceptical and to keep questioning the evidence. This is a fair approach to all behavioural, or human, or social, or natural science, or whatever the label, provided there is a claim to be scientific, or there is no disclaimer rejecting scientific standing for the work.

The second distinguishing mark of science is that the methods used in accumulating evidence are spelled out in detail. That detail enables professional colleagues to assess the merit of the work and hence to reach some agreement on whether it is credible as evidence. The detail also enables the work to be replicated. This repetition of research is rare in the social sciences. Among the few cases that have been publicised there are failures to get the same results. But where replications have confirmed the status of evidence, its power to influence has been great. In education the repeated confirmation of the relation between social class and educational opportunity is an example.

The publication of methods also enables the lay reader to ask the four key questions and to obtain some sort of answer. The scientist is accountable for the methods he uses to his audience, both lay and professional, because both need to be in a position to assess credibility before accepting the work as a basis for action.

Control over research methods and their publication for scrutiny would be unwelcome to a journalist and would ruin a good novel. Such constraint is also tiresome to social scientists who labour on the interpretive edges of the spectrum of social science. But while they work under the label of science, control and publication of methods are necessary for validation, for assessing reliability, and, above all, for giving the public a chance of assessing the dependability of their work.

Control over research methods is of course no guarantee of validity. Indeed many examples follow where the exercise of inappropriate control has invalidated evidence. But control does enable researchers to assess whether work already done is a dependable foundation on which to base new work. It enables modest predictions to be made that some new development, discovery, relationship, is liable to be found in the near future given recent evidence. What it can not do is enable scientists to say what can not be done. In 1948 the *Daily Mirror* announced that all talk of going to the moon was 'sheer balderdash'.[10] But the history of science is littered with equally dogmatic predictions that the development around the corner was impossible.

At the turn of the century Simon Newcomb was a professor of mathematics and astronomy at Johns Hopkins University, a founder and first president of the American Astronomical Society, and vice-president of the National Academy of Sciences. Among many papers he had published was one that anticipated Einstein's special theory of relativity. By analysing the relation between weight and lift he concluded, in an article titled 'The Outlook for the Flying Machine', that 'The mathematician of today admits that he can neither square the circle, duplicate the cube or trisect the angle. May not our mechanicians, in like manner, be ultimately forced to admit that aerial flight is one of that great class of problems with which man can never cope, and give up all attempts to grapple with it'.[11] This article appeared on 22 October 1903. On 17 December 1903 the Wright brothers flew their powered machine. Even three years later Newcomb was still writing that it was demonstrated that powered flight was not possible. The problem was that the Wright brothers received little publicity. The first eyewitness account to be published only appeared in 1905. It may not have been believed. It is more likely not to have been read. It appeared in the January issue of *Gleanings in Bee Culture*.[12]

CONTROVERSY 2

WHAT DO SCHOOL LEAVERS THINK ABOUT SCHOOLS?

The difficulty in arriving at reliable, valid and generalisable evidence can be best illustrated by looking at research dealing with an apparently simple question. How do teenagers leaving school look back on their schooling? Obviously there will be differences between groups of children, in different types of school, in different areas, but it should not be too difficult to select a group of, say, unskilled workers' children, from one type of school such as comprehensive, in an area such as the inner city, and to question them about their experiences and attitudes. In case there is a gap between what they say and do, the questions could be supplemented by entering schools and observing actual behaviour.

When the concern is with factual questions such as the subjects that were liked or disliked, researchers have come up with similar results for similar children. But when attitudes towards school have been investigated there has been little agreement in the evidence. In 1973, two researchers, Willis[1] in the Midlands and Scharff[2] in London, were independently looking at the same issue, transition from school to work. Each looked at working class children. The selected schools in both cases were comprehensives grown out of secondary moderns. Both worked in inner cities and all the schools had a sizeable number of black children in their intakes. Both researchers worked intensively in the schools, observing, asking questions in an unstructured, informal way, getting to know the teenagers and concentrating on their attitudes and behaviour as they prepared to leave school and enter work. In both accounts of the work the text is illustrated by quotes in the language of the children.

There is evidence from these two studies that is similar. The teachers in both areas were concerned, yet worried. The careers service is criticised in both. But the rest of the evidence presented from these two very similar studies of the same phenomena show schools that belong to different worlds. Anyone reading these two books for a description of contemporary schooling would face apparently completely conflicting evidence.

To Willis, 'The most basic, obvious and explicit dimension of counter-school culture is entrenched general and personalised opposition to "authority".'[3] The twelve lads studied made life a misery for the teachers. They were scornful of their studious peers. They opposed all that the teachers supported. The quotes from these teenagers are peppered with 'fucking' this and 'fucking' that. The teachers concerned survived only by avoiding having to maintain order. This was achieved by using discovery and individualised learning techniques to avoid overt conflict in the classroom.

There is nothing very surprising about this picture. The punch in this research of Willis is in his explanation of the way the evidence accounts for the way working class kids get working class jobs, and accept this destiny. To Willis, it is the children's own culture, own response to schooling, that prepares them for manual labour. They damn themselves into taking subordinate roles at work through their opposition to their schooling. This group may be a minority, and generalisation should be cautious. But it is a brilliant and sobering message.

However, at the same time, in similar schools, in similar urban conditions, with the same aged children, only a hundred miles to the south, Scharff, using similar methods, was reaching very different conclusions. Scharff's adolescents also seemed resistant and resentful. They also seemed to be angry. But these teenagers actually wanted to get closer to their teachers. They were willing to cooperate. In their quotes there are no four letter words. Furthermore, their anger, their surly behaviour and their protests against schooling are interpreted as symptoms of the numbness, disbelief, sense of loss felt at having to leave the school, which, deep down, is felt to be a 'mothering institution'. The teenagers here were 'mourning' their loss and responded by denying the value of their schooling.[4]

Here is a strange contrast. Was the difference due to the

selection of very different samples, one totally counter-cultural, the other totally mainstream-cultural? There is no way of knowing. Was Willis mistaken? Was that resistance to teachers really covering up the impending loss of contact with the school? Or was Scharff mistaken? Was that cooperation really covering up some profound aspect of a capitalist society? Superficially both explanations are possible. Willis examines the structure of capitalism to explain what happens in the transition from school to work. Scharff derives his explanation from an examination of human emotions at times of transition such as leaving school and entering work.

What would have happened if Scharff had looked at the lads in the Midlands? All that resentment might have been a way of concealing a genuine attachment to the school. Willis may have been misled into believing that what was said and done reflected the real selves of these teenagers. What would have happened if Willis had looked at the teenagers in London? Would those same cooperative, genteel-speaking children have been seen as subversive and foul-mouthed? It is not likely that he would have seen manifestations of mourning the loss of the school on leaving. He would probably have seen a society where a sizeable minority have only the prospect of a dead-end job and where schools perform the cooling-down of ambition that prevents revolution and even protest, and which actually ensures that the lads look forward to their future in manual labour.

By now the unfairness of these contrasts will be clear to readers who are in a position to detect that Scharff is a psychiatrist and Willis a sociologist. They may have been looking at similar situations. But each was trained in a different discipline. Each was alerted by professional practice to see different aspects of behaviour and to hear different words. Each would interpret the same data in different ways. These authors would also have had different political outlooks. Both have given accounts that may have been valid in their terms, within their theoretical frameworks. The transition from school to work may involve both mourning for the school and hatred of the school. Each could occur in the same teenager. But the unwary reader of only one of these books would get a very one-sided view of working class attitudes to school. The lay reader of both would be justifiably confused. Only when the discipline from which the researcher operates is known can the account be evaluated and the four key questions posed in the Foreword of this book be answered. This is dealt with in Chapter 2. But the reader also needs to know something of the author's view of the world and this is covered in Chapter 3. Without this knowledge there is no way of reconciling the accounts given by Scharff and Willis. Anyone wanting to help adolescents or to change their schooling, would have come to opposed conclusions if any one of these books had been read without the other, or without sufficient information on the authors, their subject discipline and their political views. This information is rarely included. Evaluating research evidence should start with a consideration of the author that could account for the conclusions drawn, regardless of the reliability of the methods used.

2

SOCIAL SCIENCE

In Chapter 1 the changing perceptions of science were discussed. Science had once been seen as the progressive completion of the jigsaw puzzle that was to become a complete picture of the natural world. Scientific method had been seen as a way of inexorably accumulating the necessary objective knowledge. But in the twentieth century science has come to be seen as interpretive, involving human explanation as well as collected facts. Science was no longer seen as only an objective, inductive activity. Instead of the anticipated progressive completion of knowledge about the natural world, science is now seen as fallible and falsifiable, a set of replaceable theories rather than a collection of unchallengeable knowledge. However, while this view of science is now common among scientists, laymen still tend to hold the older view of science as the accumulation of irrefutable fact. This of course works to the advantage of scientists. It is easier to obtain funds from a public that believes that scientific method guarantees increased understanding of the world.

The history of social science, and particularly sociology, has mirrored this changing view of science in general. There was every incentive to claim scientific status for the systematic study of human behaviour and society. It established the social sciences. Many social scientists have however consistently opposed this attempt to use methods developed for investigating the natural world, for looking at human action. First, differences between the natural and social world were being ignored. The former is changed, but not made by men. It is reality for them. The social world by contrast is made and remade as men interact with each other. Second, social scientists have to understand the bases of this active making and remaking of the world by those involved in it. Social scientists can not merely observe behaviour, they have to find out how individuals give meaning to and organise their interaction with others.

This change in emphasis in the social sciences has accelerated in the last twenty years. But many of the books, most of the theses, still give the impression of a mechanical sequence similar to the Hypothesis, Method, Observations, Conclusions sequence first met in the school science lesson. Once again there are advantages in the public holding this view, while many social scientists have moved to less recognisably 'scientific' activity. Funds and prestige are still accorded to research that is recognisably modelled on the natural sciences. But there are now many contrasting ways of collecting evidence on the human condition and these reflect contrasting theoretical positions within the social sciences. All books on research acknowledge a connection between theory and methods. But this connection is more than part of the sequence whereby theory provides the source of ideas for research and is in turn informed by the evidence collected. In practice, social science involves ways of conceiving the world and ways of finding out about it that are only separable artificially. From the start to finish of social research, the theoretical perspectives held by the researcher are influential. This applies even where the work consists only of the collection of facts on mundane subjects. It applies regardless of the prominence that is given to the theoretical context by the researcher. Whether explicit or implicit, the model of the social world held by the researcher will affect all the processes of research from deciding the precise nature of the issue to be investigated, to the way the results are written for publication.

There is nothing mystical in this idea that the collection and publication of evidence will be affected by theories about the social world. Theories are essentially ways in which social scientists make sense of the social world. They are attempts at a simplified model of that world. They are always influential because research, like any form of human interaction, is given meaning by those involved. All of us interpret our interactions with others to give them sense. Social scientists have accumulated a number of theoretical models of human behaviour. Each extends and simplifies available evidence. Conversely, these theoretical models will guide the selection of problems, procedures for collecting data, criteria for checking that the evidence is valid and ways of analysing and presenting results. The social scientist is qualified within a discipline that provides a number of such options for organising models of the social world. There is no doubt that choice made among the options will be determined by political position and persuasion. But being a functionalist or phenomenologist, behaviourist and so on, means that a specific system of organising perceptions about the social world has been adopted and that this will affect the way reality is defined, studied and reported to others. Issues of political and other bias will be discussed in Chapter 3. Here the concern is with the availability, not only of different subjects which are disciplines in the sense of laying down approaches to human behaviour, but of different approaches within each subject.

The term paradigm is usually used to describe these systems of meaning through which scientists organise their work and which incorporate not only theories for making sense of observations, but techniques for investigation, and for validating evidence. This may seem very distant from the researcher who is only interested in collecting facts about a mundane topic such as absence from school, even though it is clearly central for those who prefer comparing different societies, or institutions at different stages of development, or are happiest when theorising in armchair or seminar. But reference is always made to some model of the world in order to translate observations and measures into facts. A 90 per cent attendance rate means nothing in itself. It is given meaning once linked to other data and through the definition of attendance, absence, unjustified absence, condoned absence, truancy and so on. Social facts are created by reference to some system of meaning within social science, just as the apparently bent stick poking out of water is converted into a natural scientific fact when referred to theories of light and the concept of refraction.

The social scientist bases his claim to be saying something important on accumulated evidence and ideas. Everyone makes sense of the world through such references. The social scientist has the advantage of theories and methods which have usually been organised systematically. None of these have the stability and accumulated evidence that marks natural science paradigms, and many social scientists operate with little more than vague pictures in the mind. Those pictures will however contain insights from established theories and use evidence accumulated within often mature research traditions. In every case there is reference to some body of knowledge, some set of meanings, that enable data to be interpreted. At one end, such as experimental psychology or Keynesian economics, there will be an established tradition. At the other the social scientist may be indistinguishable from the interested layman, making sense of the world through on-the-spot, intuitive theorising.

This reference to some body of theory and evidence occurs in hypothesis-seeking as well as hypothesis-testing research. In the former, the researcher doesn't collect data at random. He sets out with a good idea of what he expects to find and this is the result of thinking about the issue in which he is interested through some model of the social world. He ends by referring the evidence collected back to that model. The hypothesis-tester has derived his hunch from some theoretical model, and refers his evidence back to it. In both cases the link to the body of theory is the hypothesis. Many researchers will vehemently deny that they either seek or test hypotheses. But social scientists are neither naive nor innocent. They are social scientists through mastering a subject and satisfying examiners in that mastery. They will report in specialist journals and to interested colleagues. Throughout the work they will discuss issues with colleagues. The research act is grounded in accumulated models of the world. If hypotheses are not made explicit they are implicit. They can be sophisticated relationships derived from fully articulated models or vague hunches that this is how social interaction works. In all cases there is some image of the social world and of the phenomena under review within it. The researcher carries into the field expectations that are influential at every stage. Any distinction between theory and method is misleading.

It is difficult to draw a verbal picture of the meaning systems, paradigms or models to which reference is made because the terms in which a description has to be made tend to be loosely and interchangeably used by social scientists. However, some understanding of the process of reference is essential for the understanding of research. A crude picture is of a number of concepts serving as bricks for a construction of a model of the social world in which theories serve as mortar to bind the concepts and link up the various sections. Concepts are the building bricks of science because they summarise experience in an organised way that is recognisable to other scientists. A concept such as social class classifies scientific knowledge about the positions of groups in relation to the means of production, or occupation, or income. The precise definition of the concept is necessary once it is used as a step towards empirical work, but even without this it is fundamental to communication between scientists. But the precision given to a concept through definition is a crucial part of the research process. The reader always needs to know whether the social class referred to is related to some concrete social position, to the subjective feelings of the respondents and so on. Concepts are the basic units of scientific activity, but they have to be put into operation in research through definitions that can lead to measurement or observation. It may be valuable to conceptualise about alienation or achievement motivation, but researching into them is tricky because no simple definition is forthcoming.

Theories can range from the grand to the humble. They can relate concepts such as education and social change. They can relate observations and measurements such as temperature and school attendance. They are often explanations of the 'if X, then Y' kind. In the natural sciences these usually take the form of laws. The volume of a gas and the pressure exerted on it are inversely proportional. Provided the correct units are used in measurement this relation has general application within specified limits. In social science there are no laws that hold across varied circumstances. Aggression may follow frustration, but Christians turn the other cheek. But theories still aid explanation. It is likely that any relation will be stated in terms of probability. 'If a school has the following characteristics, it is likely that the following attainments will be observed'. In some cases social scientists will state a hypothesis of the 'if X, then Y' kind, produce evidence to support it and then set out to test it to see if it holds up under specified conditions. Many higher degree theses are organised in this order. But most social science moves from a problem to observation or measurement without any overt deduction of a proposition which can be tested. Both Scharff[1] and Willis[2] report as if they went quickly to school to get to know more about the attitudes of adolescents towards school and work. In reality they had years of theorising behind them. Once they had collected their data, they reported their interpretations, one by reference to psychiatric theories and the other to sociological theories. The theories formulated are attempts at explanation, but clearly have no law-like status. With few exceptions, mainly in experimental psychology, human behaviour is not studied by rigid natural scientific methods, and does not aim at generalisable laws. Indeed, most of those engaged in studying humans would deny the usefulness and the ethics of controlling humans as objects of study in order to test hypotheses.

The fusion of theory and method is inevitable in the social sciences because the researcher can not know in advance whether a theory is relevant and that the data, when collected, will fit. Coleman's experience during *The Adolescent Society* study reported earlier is an example.[3] Retrospective accounts of social research contain other examples. Each social researcher is a pioneer because the data that he collects is likely to change the theoretical model that, overtly or covertly, forms the basis of the work. New data exhaust old theories. Replicating Boyle's Law is unlikely to produce anything but confirmation of the relation between the pressure and volume of a gas because all conditions can be controlled to measure the relation. But every sample of human beings is in some ways unique. There are always uncontrolled elements and these may throw up unexpected results. The loose conceptualisation, and often loose definition into observable or measurable terms in the social sciences secures the chance that established theory will prove inadequate in new investigations. This sample of working class children turn out to have higher attendance rates than that group of middle class children. The reason may turn out to be that the former contains more West Indians and they have higher attendance rates. But this was not appreciated at the start of the study and was not taken into account in the sampling. Again, the reason may be that social class as measured by parental occupation is an inadequate measure for this concept because of high unemployment in the area. Absence may turn out to be too crude. The weather may keep children away from school, or the unskilled workers' sons may prefer to attend but not go into classrooms. Indeed, in surveys where the relation between two factors such as attendance and social class are involved, the most profitable analysis often consists of introducing third factors so that the relationship can be better understood. It is when ethnic origin is introduced into the relationship between truancy and parental occupation that it becomes more meaningful. This is why social researchers often ask for standard variables such as social class, sex, age and ethnic origin. They enable some control to be exercised over the factors under investigation and lead to better understanding of their relation.

It is misleading to talk of 'social science' for two reasons. First, many who practise it reject the label 'science'. They reject the naturalism of scientific activity. To them the social world can not be understood through the senses, through observation and measurement. To them an idealistic, rationalistic approach is needed. Second, even within those who claim to be scientists there are great divisions. These are not just boundaries between Economics, Psychology, Sociology and so on. They are disputes within each of these subjects. Within sociology for example we have functionalists conceiving the social world in biological terms and Marxists seeing it in terms of inevitable social upheaval following economic change. These two schools may be in conflict, but most of those within each share the same approach to enquiry. They are positivistic in using natural scientific methods and in looking for causes and laws. Opposed to them, but equally divided on other grounds, are sociologists who see humans not as objects of enquiry, but as thinkers who act in a motivated way that must be understood. It is their thoughts, motives and meanings that matter, not the theories of social scientists. Instead of putting men into some model of the social world, these sociologists put men at the centre. The science is in the interpretation of these individual interpretations.

The most remarkable change in conceptualisation and methods of enquiry has taken place in criminology. Early investigations looked for relations between crime and social conditions such as poverty, the business cycle and bad housing. Later, the focus was on broken homes, delinquent sub-cultures, differential association and relationships between children and their parents. In the investigation of these associations between crime and aspects of social organisation, the methods used were largely comparisons between delinquents and non-delinquents, matched to ensure that extraneous factors were not intervening to cause the crime, rather than those being investigated. But however large the size of the control groups, however careful the matching, the results became no more convincing. When Sheldon and Eleanor Glueck carried out their control group study of 500 delinquents matched with 500 non-delinquents for *Unravelling Juvenile Delinquency*, there was little point in pushing this line of enquiry any further.[4] This study was the triumph of positivist criminology, having statistically uncovered the major causes of crime. Ironically at this time Lemert and others were turning delinquency studies on their head.[5] Now it was the way society defined crime and labelled criminals that was subject to investigation. Becker expressed this view as follows, '. . . social groups create deviance by making the rules whose infraction constitutes deviance'.[6] To look at this process social scientists had to listen to those labelled as well as those doing the labelling. There could be no matching of delinquent and non-delinquent, for there were now no criminals, only groups stigmatised through definitions of criminality and the attachment of labels to them as fitting the definition. Instead of observing the criminal, the interest was in the way the public, police and courts created delinquents.

There is rarely a clear-cut divide between the different protagonists within social science in practice. Each researcher is likely to draw on a variety of traditions. In sociology each major tradition has an enduring history. Functionalism as a model of the social world, and positivism as an approach to enquiry dominated the subject in this century up to the 1960s, but since then social phenomenology, symbolic interactionism and many other schools putting 'man back at the centre' have been ascending. In psychology the study of behaviour by experimental methods has been deeply entrenched. But there has always been an alternative school stressing the importance of human activity directed through the meanings given to the situation by the subject, not produced by some external stimulus. The image of behaviouristic, experimental psychology was an immobilised dog festooned with wires, salivating as bells were rung, or shocks were applied, and food offered. The image of the newer ethogenic perspective is of the researcher, dressed in jeans and supporter's scarf, listening to the chanting and banter behind the home side's goal at a football match.

These two extremes account for many of the criticisms of social science. The behaviour of rats in mazes, or of immobilised dogs seems dubiously relevant to humans. Experiments on leadership, observation schedules on classroom interaction between teachers and pupils, and surveys of attitudes of teachers towards sensitive issues such as corporal punishment, often seem unreal, or incomplete. This is a very proper critique of validity, however impressionistic it may seem to the social scientists being criticised. At the other extreme, studies where the researcher has joined a gang, sat in classrooms or befriended adolescents in youth clubs ring true to laymen. But these studies are impressionistic and are rightly criticised as telling the layman what he already knows, or which could be more clearly expressed by a journalist.

There is a disturbing parallel between the internal conflicts within the social sciences and the criticisms of the laymen outside. Constructing models of the social world, testing hypotheses and approximating to controlled experimentation has produced impressive evidence over the last century. But little of it has survived for long and much of it is now looked on as ludicrous. The lay criticism that those stages of development, those flow diagrams and those differential equations don't look like anything human, isn't far from the criticism levelled by social scientists who maintain that the human, social script is not written for people, but by them. This is unwelcome criticism for social scientists. For example, at the 1970 annual meeting of the British Sociological Association, when the 'new' Sociology of Education was launched, there was one critical paper by Bantock pointing to the similarities between sociology and literary criticism.[7] All the papers read at this conference have been published in a number of books. But Bantock's paper was not published with any of them. Yet the parallel with literary criticism has since been repeated by other authors, and the comparison is now accepted without demur. The simile and the metaphor tend to be the tools of both literary critic and interpretive social scientists.

The production of 'accounts' by the individual being studied smacks of realism. They suggest the way that people make sense, and make bearable, their lot in the social world. But 'telling it as it is', in the words of these involved, does not explain how reality has been constructed. This explanation has to be worked out by the researcher. At that point the difference between journalist, or novelist and social scientist is the discipline they do or do not exercise. This makes it essential for the social scientist to spell out the methods used, the assumptions behind those methods and to do this in a language that is easily understood by the reader and which will enable him to answer the three key questions stated earlier. Curiously, the attempt to reproduce the worlds of the people being investigated is often contained in explanatory linking passages that are esoteric beyond the point of intelligibility.

The reader of social science research has a problem that goes beyond the need to decide the reliability and validity of the evidence reported. There is still the need to assess the strength with which the professionals concerned are protecting the boundaries of their discipline. This is a feature of all professions. The confident face presented to the public contrasts with the uncertainty when the same professional discusses the patient, the case, the client or the research with colleagues. Indeed, there is an uncomfortable similarity between the undecipherable doctor's prescription and the unintelligible research report. Both sustain the boundary between professional and public.

The maintenance of a boundary around a professional community enables the stamp of approval to be given within. But it also allows a degree of confidence to be maintained by the professional in his dealings with the public that diminishes between peers. The broadcast, book and article in a newspaper or popular journal ooze confidence. The seminar, academic paper and lecture are titled 'pilot', 'provisional' or 'an approach to'. Keynesian and Monetarist economists confidently broadcast opposed views, and neither would have much in common with a supporter of Social Credit. Yet all three schools have the ear of governments. The failure of economists to explain, or predict, or agree among themselves is no barrier to sustaining prestige and audience. The disputes within economics are as marked as those within psychology or sociology. Indeed, underlying these disputes in all the social sciences is the same problem of the complexity of social life and the polarisation between those who try to retain the view of individuals controlling their own interactions, and those who model the social world in order to use the quantitative methods associated with natural science.

Here is Schoeffler describing the failure of economists to retain the humanity, in all its annoying unpredictability, of human behaviour.[8] 'They artificially mechanize, artificially simplify, artificially generalize, artificially fixate, artificially factorize, artificially close, artificially semiclose, and artificially isolate. They employ an artificial indirectness. They assume the heterogeneous to be homogeneous, the complex to be simple, the complexly related to be simply related, the unknown to be known, the variable to be fixed, the open to be closed, the connected to be isolated and the indeterminate to be determinate.'

Economists tend to model the world without reference to human idiosyncracies. The focus is on generalised behaviour, not on the actual way in which individuals respond to shortages of cash or to tax arrangements, or to rises in prices, or to any other features of everyday life that require economic decisions. On the test of ability to predict, economists have a poor record. If prediction was reliable, economists could confidently work the stock market. In practice this remains the preserve of amateur, but mainly rich stockbrokers.

The tension between synthesising to approach the rigour of the natural sciences and trying to preserve the natural activity of man while observing them is inevitable while the label science is attached to the study of societies, groups or individuals. Balancing detachment and involvement is the lot of social researchers. They are influenced by their subjects and simultaneously influence them. Unless the researcher is satisfied with observing behaviour without consideration of the meaning behind it he has to treat subjective meanings in an objective way. To Rickman, understanding, the process of getting to know the thoughts, feelings and motives of other humans, is involved in every stage of social scientific enquiry.[9] It enters into the formulation of hypotheses, whether as the basis for the research or its product, the collection of data, or its interpretation. The natural scientist can abstract, relate, experiment and analyse without having to explain why gases act as they do. The social scientist is continually involved in interpretation. He is part of the situation he is investigating, and that investigation requires him to ask 'why'. This is why social research is not mechanical. The creative stages which precede and follow the standard procedures of enquiry are largely interpretive and imaginative.

The divisions between those aiming to approximate to the methods of natural sciences and those aiming to preserve the natural condition of those studied are also present inside all the social sciences. Experimental psychology may have been dominant across this century, but there have always been psychologists who claim that action can not be reduced to measurable, simplified behaviour that is reproducible under controlled experimental conditions. Scientistic approaches are contrasted with ethogenic, where the observation of real life situations and the accounts of those observed are substituted for experimentation.[10]

It is the human facility for acting rationally and controlling interactions that can obstruct the social scientist bent on obtaining insights into behaviour. It can never be assumed that the observed behaviour is not a front deliberately erected as a response to the present of the researcher. But researchers are also human. Consciously or not they also interpret the events that they are observing. In their field work they have to interpret and record the action, and particularly the language of those being investigated. This means getting to know the conventions of the group in order to understand the meanings they are giving to situations. This interpretation involves both the use of language and of everyday meanings. In many cases it means interpreting what the subjects of the investigation meant, or what those who reported the behaviour of others meant. Just as the historian is necessarily involved in assessing the real meaning of documentary evidence from another age, so the social scientist is involved in sorting out the meaning of what has been seen, written or said. Both have to ask about the meaning to the persons being studied, to others who collected the information together and to themselves as they sort it out in a meaningful way. At each stage a person involved in one culture, one class, one period of time, may have to give meaning to words spoken or written in others.

Cicourel emphasises that it has been rare for social scientists to examine this stage of interpretation.[11] But the crucial question is why was that meaning given to that act at that time and in that place. This is by no means a universally held view of priorities in social research, but it is less dangerous than the assumption that human behaviour is open to controlled scientific investigation. Reliability in social science can often only be achieved at the cost of validity. Interpretation can be excluded by rigid design of the investigation but in doing so any relevance to everyday life is likely to be lost.

Humans, whether as researchers or subjects, also engage actively in the research process, reducing the extent of control. When a physicist observes the volume of a gas as the pressure exerted on it is altered with the temperature held constant, he can refer his observations to those of many others in a much repeated experiment. But the units for measuring volume, pressure and temperature are defined in advance and used by successive experimenters. As a scientist he uses definitions which relate his findings to those of innumerable other scientists. Furthermore, the limits of temperature and pressures within which the volume of a gas remains inversely proportional to the pressure exerted on it have also been determined by repeated experiment. The social scientist by contrast has often to prune or distort his observations to fit into his conceptual boxes. Some will just not fit, for the data is the product of human interaction, not scientific definition and control.

There is therefore a gap between the ambitious, abstract theorising of some social scientists and the modest data collected from numerous small-scale studies of concrete situations. Rarely do the latter illuminate the former. Indeed, it is unusual for the speculative theories about the human condition to be phrased in a way that could be verified through research. Frequently the concepts are so abstract that they could never be defined in a way that would enable their interrelation to be tested. Glaser and Strauss have seen the answer in grounded theory which is developed during, not in advance of, investigation.[12] This is an attack on speculation not theory, an attempt to give it substance, not to challenge its importance. Grounded theory is an attempt to bridge the gap that is the central concern of this book. It avoids the common divorce between abstract theorising and the evidence from actual investigation.

At the centre of the debate within the social sciences over appropriate methods of research is the concept of objectivity. This is central to the natural sciences. The scientist uses methods that minimise the influence of his own feelings and views on what is observed. He accepts controls over his own behaviour during the research and he controls the initiation of the behaviour observed, and its context. But many social scientists reject this approach. To them the objectivity is apparent, not real. The social scientist does not impose a neutral research design that enables him to observe behaviour and get answers to questions that are genuine responses. In practice he imposes his own preconceptions, and these may bear little resemblance to the situation as conceived by those actually involved. The objectivity is superficial and has distorted the picture obtained. The researcher obtains information that is a reflection of the design that he has used and which has been determined by his own anticipations of what will be found.

The distinction between approaches to research that stress the need to follow the procedures shown to be productive within the natural sciences, and those that maintain that this produces only a fallacious objectivity is developed in Chapter 9. But it has to be remembered when reading the intervening chapters. In writing about techniques of collecting information there is a danger of divorcing them from the theoretical positions that underlie them. Research designs reflect theoretical perspectives. Those interested in uncovering the meaning given to events by pupils, or young workers, or delinquents, will use very different methods to those interested in structures, roles and norms, or in answers to questions. The latter are not just being shortsighted, nor the former just ignoring the organisations and social arrangements that persist while individual interpretations of situations change. Each is researching in a fashion directed by a particular social scientific perspective that highlights different aspects. It is common sense that each aspect must be closely related. Many social scientists work to reconcile the different models. But the models still determine the methods because theories and methods are indivisible.

CONTROVERSY 3

SHOULD SCIENTISTS INVESTIGATE SENSITIVE SOCIAL PROBLEMS?

The conventional view of science is of detached pursuit of knowledge. In practice, the personal involvement of the scientist in the issues he investigates increases as they become of pressing public concern. It is not just that the scientist will be exposed to personal as well as professional criticism, but that attacks on his personal motives for undertaking the work will be extended to challenge his competence as a scientist.

In 1969 Jensen reviewed the literature on racial and social class differences in intelligence.[1] This was followed by another issue of the *Harvard Educational Review* devoted to critiques of his views[2] and a further issue containing his replies to his critics.[3] With the explosive racial situation in the USA Jensen's suggestion that there were innate differences in the distribution of measured intelligence between races was sure to cause an uproar. But three points stand out in the ensuing dispute. First, many thought the subject should never have been investigated. Second, there were vitriolic attacks on the personal integrity of Jensen. Third, his standing as a psychologist was challenged. Similar criticisms were later made of his supporters in Britain.

The Jensen report was used by segregationists in the Southern States of the USA to justify existing inequalities in education.[4] Jensen, however, maintained that he was trying to develop a new theory of intelligence that would hold more hope for successful compensatory education, thus helping ethnic minorities. Brazziel, however, claimed that the *Harvard Educational Review* had acted irresponsibly in publishing evidence that would inevitably be misunderstood and used to sustain inequality.[5] Another critic maintained that to raise the issue at all was racism.[6]

In this dispute personal abuse was mixed with academic criticism. Jensen was likened to Governor Wallace, was accused of supporting the idea of Negro inferiority and of justifying school segregation.[7] When the National Foundation for Educational Research decided to include an article by Jensen in *Educational Research* it was attacked for its racialist content, but also for the pseudo-scientific nature of the evidence produced even before the actual article was published.[8] The validity of the evidence was challenged in advance. The National Foundation was accused of 'elevating a bogus and largely discredited thesis into respectibility'.[9] The acting director of the National Foundation replied that it would have been prejudice and censorship not to publish a contribution from such a distinguished psychologist.[10]

More fuel had been added to this dispute by the publication in Britain of a book by Eysenck before the furore over the original Jensen article had died down.[11] Here a serious social and academic issue was virtually reduced to farce by the conflicting critics.[12] The author, a refugee from Hitler's Europe, was accused of Fascism. Methodological errors bordering on lunacy were suggested and terms like ignorant and impudent abounded. Eysenck was accused of playing into the hands of politicians, of disregarding the work of environmentalists and of being unscientific and unscholarly. Unfortunately this apparent incompetence was seen to be combined with an effortless, masterly and persuasive style that would too easily capture the imagination of the intelligent plain man.[13] Academic incompetence, a lack of personal integrity and a facility to seduce the public were seen as combined.

The only way the plain man can cut through this animosity is to wait until the original controversy has died down. Thus Bodmer and Cavalli-Sforza in a calm review of the evidence over a year after the publication of Jensen's original article concluded that the currently available evidence was inadequate to resolve the question in either direction.[14] They agree that in the present climate of opinion the chances of misinterpretation of the evidence are so high that publication inevitably increased racial tensions. Above all they saw many more useful biological problems for the scientist to tackle that could lead to more conclusive answers and more fruitful action.

This balanced view contrasts with the emotion generated earlier.

First, there is no accusation of stupidity, personal malice or political reaction. When controversial subjects are investigated the scientist runs the risk of being labelled not only as a Fascist or a Communist, but as an imbecile. Second, the priority given to the research is judged against alternative possibilities, not against the political climate. The danger of accusing publishers of airing disruptive views is that it can lead to censorship. The liberal critics of Jenson and Eysenck were themselves under attack from more radical social scientists who saw the need, not to stop at criticism, but to convert social science into action against an unfair situation.[15] With such diverse views the struggle might focus on who had the right to censor, not on the quality of the articles presented for publication.

Perhaps the most alarming aspect of this controversy was its value as news. It was reported in newspapers and popular magazines as well as academic journals. In all there was some discussion of the reliability of the methods used in collecting the evidence. This unusual concern with reliability occurs only when accepted views are challenged. It acts as another pressure on the scientist when choosing his research area. When the reward may be recognition by some colleagues and the hatred of others; when personal integrity, political belief and professional competence are likely to be discussed in public, and when brief, often distorted versions are to reappear through the mass media, the scientist is no longer a detached observer. It is a brave man who will expose his work to both the microscope and the hatchet.

In the chapter that follows, the personal and political, as well as the professional pressures on authors are considered. These are important determinants of what is researched and how the results are presented and interpreted. But there is no sign that the contestants in the nature–nurture dispute are shy of being involved in a public wrangle. Jensen ensured that the article which caused all the fuss in the *Harvard Educational Review* was available to the press in advance.[16] J. S. Coleman, whose analyses of White Flight were received as yet another attack on policies to achieve racial equality, is similarly prone to ensure maximum publicity. Eysenck carries on his arguments in letters to the national press. Indeed, he and Rose, the co-author of the National Union of Teachers pamphlet[17] to counter the Jenson and the Eysenck views, seem to produce a double-act whenever the issue comes into the public domain.[18]

The most striking manifestation of this public exposure of usually private scientific dispute has been the attacks on the later work of the late Cyril Burt.[19] These attacks have not only implied bias, but fraud. There is probably no way in which the truth about the bases of Burt's last articles can be discovered. The evidence was published, but there is mystery around both how it could have been produced, and over who did the work. The affair reveals a most disturbing limitation on social research. Given an established reputation, a researcher can produce apparently credible evidence that will convince his academic peers. Now examples of fraud from the natural sciences are included in this book. But the chances of any dramatic revelation that is not based on sound research is slim where the resources needed are expensive, where there are usually teams involved, where replication is possible and where many other researchers are working in the same field. In the social sciences the one-man research effort is still common, replication is rarely possible or attractive, and researchers are reluctant to allow their data to be used by others. The chances of fraud increase when scientific activity goes on in private.

The practical consequences of this controversy over race and intelligence have been as unpredictable as the academic. Affirmative discrimination in the United States led to the Bakke case where failure to obtain a university place because of a quota of blacks was successfully challenged. Intelligence tests have been banned in New York, Philadelphia and Washington D.C., even though they are a means of benefiting the able poor. Desegregation of schools, and bussing to obtain an agreed ethnic mix, have led to a 'white flight' which has exacerbated the situation that was supposed to be remedied. In Britain, positive discrimination policy has been muted. But the urge to oppose racialism is still strong. In 1978, for example, the National Union of Teachers produced a pamphlet, *Race, Education, Intelligence*, to instruct teachers on the evidence available.[20] The pamphlet attacks 'scientific racism' and includes in this all attempts to investigate the nature–nurture question. Indeed, the authors argue that 'We must therefore seriously question the intention of those who persist in asking this question and attempt to give it scientific status'. Thus anyone pursuing such research is under suspicion of being racist. Curiously however the pamphlet concludes that 'More than 94 per cent of all genetic differences between individuals that have been studied occur between individuals of the *same* "race", not *between* "races".'[21] Scientific accuracy is produced by the prosecution, but denied the defence.

This controversy rumbles on. It is probable that the nature–nurture debate is so complicated that it is a waste of resources to try to sort it out. But it will be argued repeatedly in this book that a priority for social researchers is to probe the differences between what people assume is happening and what is actually happening. It is necessary to keep this debate alive because failure to do so is liable to penalise just those minority groups whom teachers and others are anxious to help. The well-meaning have a habit of further penalising the poor. That is why social science is essential. Social conditions change, and social policies that run on are liable to start having adverse effects. Positive discrimination in Britain, initially just and possibly beneficial, may now be both unfair on teachers and unhelpful to pupils.[22] It is unwise to be dogmatic about the implications of evidence from the social sciences because the context to which they are applied is liable to change fast.

3

QUESTIONS OF AUTHOR, SUBJECT AND DATE

Authors have a variety of motives for writing. They have in common only a desire to spread information, exert influence and gain material rewards or prestige. The first major distinction is between books and articles that are attempts to produce reliable evidence and those that reflect only the views of the author. The presence of references to research results is no guarantee of objectivity. Flat-earthers have no difficulty accumulating convincing evidence. Lunatic theories of human behaviour are even easier to support by dependable-looking evidence.

A further distinction has to be made between books and articles in popular journals such as *New Society* or *Forum* and research papers published in journals for professionals such as the *British Journal of Psychology* or *Sociology*. Not only does the technical level of these articles differ, but so do the motives of the authors. Books and popular articles tend to be written as collections of work that has already appeared in professional journals. The writer of a book is paid by the publisher. In the social, as in the natural sciences, prestige is as likely to be lost as much as gained through the effort at reaching a wide audience. Whereas a research paper for fellow professionals is designed to advance existing knowledge about events or techniques, and must include sufficient description of methods to enable the readers to assess its reliability, a book or popular article tends to include only enough method to indicate how the information was obtained. Finally, fellow professionals are assumed to have read the literature relevant to the subject and all that is required is the shorthand of a few references. But a book or more popular article has to summarise and simplify this background material.

A most alarming development is the proliferation of 'readers' presenting extracts from a number of sources on a subject. Another is the production of simple, filleted versions for students. These present the core of the original without any accompanying description of methods and their shortcomings which appear in the original. No opportunity or invitation is given to assess reliability or validity. Students and public fed on a diet of readers and popular accounts would have little idea of the real nature of social science.

The real world of the social researcher

The assessment of social research requires a realistic image of the researcher. Because he is interested in social relationships he is liable to have strong views about them. The motive for research is often to promote change. For example, Lacey, starting out on his research later published as 'Hightown Grammar', reports receiving contradictory advice.[1] One set of colleagues advised a conventional detached view of schooling, but another group advised him to set about taking the lid off the grammar schools. Few social scientists now claim to be value-free. In practice scientists strive in directions and within limits established by the communities within which they work. The true and the valuable are not absolute standards, but are related to current scientific belief and practice. Natural science is not value-free, but permeated with values that each scientist learns as he becomes a fully accepted practitioner, as well as with personal opinions.

The attack on the idea of value-free social science has been sustained and bitter. However, it has only been resisted as an attack on the status of social science, but has rarely penetrated the screen between professional and layman. The dispute can be found in a polite form in academic journals and in bitter disputes at professional conferences, but the only public battle has been expressed as part of the student revolt, where swingeing attacks have been made on sociology in particular as imbued with bourgeois values and defensive attitudes.[2]

To Gouldner, the idea of value-free sociology is a group myth, a caste mark of the decorous.[3] It enables sociologists to be morally indifferent, to escape responsibility for the implications of their work and to escape from the world into academic security. To Mills it has enabled abstracted empiricism to dominate research activity so that sociologists can become fact-gatherers for administrators and can ignore important political issues.[4]

The consequences of the persistence of the value-free myth can be seen first in the wasteful proliferation of elaborate analyses of dubious data from questionnaires churned out by computers, which, as Runciman has pointed out, have produced nothing comparable in importance to the insights of classical social theorists.[5] These empirical studies supporting the ceilings of archive rooms in university libraries are often studies of the attitudes of students, the applications of new statistical techniques and comparisons of unlikely subjects such as primary education in Pimlico and eastern Tasmania. Each has contributed little to the sum of knowledge or the truth, but has qualified its author for membership of his community of peers by showing that he has learned the necessary procedures of research and reporting.

Gouldner has stressed the importance of this issue as follows:

> The problem of value-free sociology has its most poignant implications for the social scientist in his role as educator. If sociologists ought not to express their personal views in the academic setting then how are students to be safeguarded against the unwitting influence of these values which shape the sociologist's selection of problems, his preferences for certain hypotheses or conceptual schemes, his neglect of others? For these are unavoidable and, in this sense, there is and can be no value-free sociology.[6]

The second impact of values comes in the selection and survival of evidence until it virtually becomes part of the mythology of a subject. The Hawthorne studies have wide currency in the social sciences and subjects using such evidence.[7] But the original work has been strongly criticised. First, the conclusions on the superiority of good human relations over material conditions and monetary rewards do not seem related to the evidence produced. Second, the frailty of the evidence does not seem to justify the survival of the conclusions. The Hawthorne studies and the human relations movement they initiated were supports for, and were supported by, the prevailing climate of capitalism and democracy. Workers could be kept contented by democratic means.

A similar case is the Lewin, Lippitt and White experiments on different teaching climates.[8] Here the frequently reported results again support democratic leadership. But one of the original research workers has explained how he and his fellow students put their all into the democratic but not into the authoritarian or *laissez-faire* role.[9] They were experimenting while Hitler was still a menace. They were involved in a violently anti-authoritarian period. But this climate has survived and accounts for the selective survival reported earlier.

The frequency with which both these experiments appear in textbooks can be explained by the support they give to paramount values in our culture. Both studies were an outstanding contribution to the development of social science. They are more reliable than most. Their fragility is unfortunate, but the selective nature of their survival is even more disturbing.

The researcher also faces problems in organising and publishing his work. It has to be financed. Access has to be obtained from organisations. Individuals have to be persuaded to cooperate. Government departments, advisers, inspectors and sponsoring bodies have to be satisfied that the work is worthwhile and the researcher trustworthy. Personal relations in research teams have to be kept amicable. Platt has listed ten points where practical, personal and organisation problems can affect work.[10] There are now accounts of the trials and tribulations of researchers. Platt's work was based on interviews with social scientists. Bell and Newby,[11] and Shipman[12] have edited accounts of the experiences of researchers as they went about their work. These books and Hammond's *Sociologists at Work*[13] contrast sharply with the conventional 'do it yourself' text on research methods.

The picture that emerges from books on the process of social research is of enthusiasm, hard work, ingenuity, and perhaps a touch of acrimony. Dale describes the research load as involving two days' work in one.[14] He reports crises and periods of doubt, but twenty-six years of work around his subject have still left a thirst to find out more. John and Elizabeth Newson show how the birth of their own child focused their attention on child-rearing.[15] Later their punched cards, schedules and letters stack up in their living room. They describe this early work as a cottage industry. Bell reports on disagreements within the team studying Banbury and on unforeseen difficulties leading to delays in publication.[16] Ford looks back at her earlier research and sees someone floating a counter-rumour because of her disgust and fright at the replacement of one form of overt injustice within education by another was more subtle and tenacious.[17] All through these accounts there are signs of strain, of over-work overcome by enthusiasm. Douglas finds the weight of data in longitudinal studies creating the need for painful decisions to be made in order to get the evidence published.[18] After twenty-eight years with the study he remains convinced of its importance. The Newsons have to choose between the many demands on their services as their work produces more and more evidence. These researchers paint a personal picture of research as a human activity. Perhaps the image for the reader is of Dale, seriously ill for six months, trying to catch up in the face of assistants who administered tests wrongly, or tests that failed to arrive from the printers, a typing bar falling off the computer output, of programming problems and of mounting piles of data. Dale gives a picture of immersion in the work, 'during walks, driving the car, in bed at night, over the endless cups of tea in the study . . .'.[19] Preoccupied in this way he nearly falls under the hooves of four cart horses pulling a brewer's dray.

The researcher's problems do not end when the evidence has been produced. It still has to be published. As Becker has pointed out, there is an irreducible conflict between the view of the researcher and those he studies. Research is deflating, generalising and abstracting. Someone is going to feel insulted, even if others will feel comforted. Most researchers have experienced the twinges of conscience as they write critically about those who have allowed them access, answered their questions and taken them into their confidence. Problems can also arise within research teams over what should be published. Every researcher writes in the context of such minor or major dilemmas. These are not as dramatic as the publication of the Pentagon papers, but the reader should recognise that researchers usually face tough decisions. They do not want to appear parasitic, biters of the hands that fed them coffee, nor to queer the pitch for those that follow. Yet they feel obliged to report honestly, and there is mileage in revelation.

The date of publication

In the 1970 general election in Britain the failure of the pollsters was proportional to the span of time which elapsed between the last survey and election day.[20] Opinion Research Centre was nearest the actual result and completed its fieldwork last. Marplan was farthest out and completed its fieldwork soonest. It is rare for a few days to make such a difference, but there is always a need to consider the year in which a work was published. This stems partly from the accumulation of books on library shelves and on book lists, and partly from the mechanics of writing and publishing. Books are removed to reserve stacks of libraries because of shortage of shelf space rather than redundancy. Book lists supplied to students tend to be antiquated not only through infrequent amendment, but the tendency of tutors to keep recommending books which they possess and have found useful in the past, or even written themselves. This combination of academic inertia, sentimentality and even greed results in a need to examine the date of publication in relation to developments within the subject disciplines.

Ageing is not the only danger. Books are reprinted frequently, particularly in paperback, but revised rarely. A glance through the dates of reprints to the last date of revision or original date of publication is particularly necessary in popular books. Furthermore, publishing is a slow process. There is often an eighteen-month delay between an article for an academic journal in the social sciences being accepted and its publication. A book takes a similar time to produce from the acceptance of the typescript. A glance at the preface will often give the date of completion by the author which is usually at least a year before the date of publication. Some academic journals give the date when the typescript was received.

In this type of article or book considered here there is a further complication. The evidence on which they have been based may have been collected long before the work was published. Books are often adapted from higher degree theses or from articles based on field work done in the past. A further step, therefore, is to find out when the evidence was collected. Thus books on child development still draw on work done in the 1920s. Hemming's study of

Problems of Adolescent Girls was published in 1960, but based on letters written to a magazine between 1953 and 1955.[21] Tapper's study of political socialisation, *Young People and Society*, was published in 1971 with the Labour Party in opposition, and based on information collected just after the defeat of the Conservative Party in 1964.[22] The transition from hard to soft cover is also slow. The study by Hargreaves of *Social Relations in a Secondary School* was published as hardback in 1967 and paperback in 1970.[23] The fieldwork was done in 1963 and 1964. By the time three follow-up studies directed by J. W. B. Douglas dealing with children under five,[24] primary schooling,[25] and experience up to school leaving or the threshold of the sixth form[26] were published, their subjects had reached the ages respectively of twelve, eighteen and twenty-two. It must be remembered that these books are among the most reliable as they do include and describe the sources of their evidence. Where this is missing, the reader is left to guess how relevant the information still is.

A rare example of clear presentation of the historical development of a research project which also is refreshingly free of didactic deadpan is the published account of the work of the Sociological Research Unit.[27] Here the attempts to obtain finance in 1962, final success and start in 1964, through to finish at Christmas 1967 are described. Significantly, this monograph, published in 1970, also includes reports of breakdowns, changes of direction and warnings of possible unreliability.

Another reason for watching the date of publication refers to the redundancy of words rather than events. Social change is accompanied by changes in the meanings of words. To call someone liberal, gay or high may be complimentary one year but insulting the next. Jewish in 1939 indicated pacific and defensive. In 1970 it implied militant and aggressive. In education the term secondary used to mean the selective school before 1944, but non-selective as well thereafter. A technical college no longer means primarily evening classes, but a variety of mainly daytime courses. Scripture becomes religious instruction and then religious education. But these are only the obvious changes. Words are part of a continually changing set of symbols employed by men to communicate. The changes are as subtle but as persistent as the changes in the life the words express. An author assumes that his words can bring a picture to the reader's mind. But once time has passed the same word may produce a different picture. Yesterday's survey becomes history. Yesterday's words refer to a different world.

It is also advisable to determine the audience for whom the book was written and the place where the evidence was collected. Psychology and sociology still tend to be dominated by American texts. Yet in these, and subjects like education, it may be misleading to draw conclusions about British organisations and social relations from American experience. Again the crucial area is the collection of evidence. It should be noted in advance if the children whose development has been used for illustration were Viennese or American, that the educational system, social background, economy, history, language or politics are alien and therefore that generalisations may be misleading.

E. H. Carr has argued that this perspective can be illustrated from the study of history where it is necessary to study first the historical and social environment of the historian, then to investigate the bees that are buzzing under this particular historian's bonnet.[28] Only then can the reader have any idea of why the material designated as facts in the work came to be selected. Thus the facts of history are continually being amended as the context within which the historian works itself changes.

The speed of educational change makes it difficult to detect these changes from books and few can follow the accounts of research in academic journals. Hence there is a lag in new perspectives reaching the non-specialist reader and a danger that even a book written in the last decade may be misleading. An examination of reading lists for students on education courses will show many such cases. Thus two popular anthropological studies in paperback by Margaret Mead, *Coming of Age in Samoa*, published in 1929,[29] and *Growing Up in New Guinea*, published in 1931, appear on most lists.[20] In both cases there remain paperback editions still being printed. These books may never have been accepted by professional anthropologists but are widely used to illustrate that patterns of upbringing differ between cultures and that it is possible for children to move smoothly through adolescence without much discipline and without emotional disturbance. Yet later writers have shown that it is easy for

Western anthropologists to miss the real discipline of life in an apparently easygoing, simple society.[31] Generations of students have obtained a picture of life under the palms that would probably be unrecognisable to those actually lying there.

A final example from criminology will illustrate the same point that rapid advances in subject knowledge leave a residue on bookshelves that is misleading. The main historical interest in criminology has been in the reasons why laws were broken. This focused attention largely on working class youth. The first refocusing came in 1940 when Sutherland published his study of white collar crime and showed that it was the definition of what constituted a crime that mattered.[32] Much of contemporary criminology had developed this idea so that the focus is on why particular actions by particular groups of persons are labelled at particular times as crimes, rather than on why unchanging and agreed standards of behaviour are violated. Crime is seen as an interaction between groups in which those with power label some actions of those without as criminal.[33]

Pressures on the author

Authors and researchers are subject to a variety of pressures as they select, plan, implement and report their work. The mildest yet most widespread in the social sciences is that involvement during research reduces detachment and the intricacies, idiosyncrasies, loves and hates of those studied come to be appreciated. Social scientists visiting schools, hospitals or factories for a brief visit and the quick application of an interview programme or questionnaire tend to give a cold, clinical and usually critical account. Participant observers come to see the difficulties faced by the teachers, the nurses or the workers. Their reports tend to be warm and any criticism is tempered by allowances due to adverse conditions. This is a crude generalisation, but it is important to look at the extent to which the writer involved himself and got interested in the human problems as well as the working efficiency of his subjects.

Authors are, however, often pressing a cause and their bias may not be eliminated by the research design. In education there are pressure groups supporting comprehensive schools, public schools, streaming and de-streaming. These groups are vocal, organised and eager to produce results that will support their case. The obvious clues are to be found in the publishers or sponsoring bodies. Political parties and societies, religious organisations and pressure groups publish or sponsor useful but slanted books and pamphlets. This information is often on the title page or in the preface. It is worth while to get to know the views of some of the associations with the largest output. Thus the Fabian Society in supporting the collective solution to social problems and the Institute of Economic Affairs in its support for private enterprise are pressing particular political beliefs though they may claim only to approve publications and not to influence the authors. The *Critical Quarterly* and the *New-Left Review* find no difficulty in accumulating evidence to support their conflicting cases.

Even where there are no obvious sources of bias, there is still a need to study the professional and social pressures on the author. No scientist can escape these pressures, for the natural sciences require increasingly large sums of money and this tends to deflect research into channels approved by government or industry. Many eminent American social scientists joined Project Camelot after it received 6 million dollars from the US Army.[34] This was later terminated by the President of the United States when its objectives and political implications became suspect. Among the motives for joining was the attraction of belonging to a wealthy project close to the centre of power, a hope that the US Army could be humanised and deflected into constructive work, and even an honest admission that the money was good. But the cost of association was the taint of involvement in a project which was concerned with uncovering data on the causes of revolutions, for use by the US Army.

A more important restraint comes through controls exercised over individuals by the discipline of their subject. Undergraduate and graduate education immerses the student in books, lectures, tutorials and research procedures that are chosen and controlled by teaching or supervisory staff. Getting a place and a grant for a second degree or to do research usually means fitting in to the field of interests of existing faculty members. Getting an article published depends on the attitudes of established men who act as editors or referees. In this way each subject exerts control over its members and it becomes a discipline. Hagstrom has argued that within scientific communities in the natural sciences any disputes that do arise are limited by the actions of those controlling publicity, so that the majority remain working in areas where there is agreement and students are given an image of unified contents and procedures.[35]

Some ideas of the conventions governing science can be gauged from Merton's view that the stress in science on advancing knowledge puts a premium on original contribution.[36] Rewards go to those who discover first, not only in the form of Nobel prizes, but through giving a name to a substance or process, thus bestowing immortality on men like Boyle, Mendel, Pavlov and Zeigarnik. This emphasis on originality often clashes with the other main stress in science on organised scepticism and objectivity. For most scientists, getting into print is a sufficient reward, symbolising originality, even if the reality was a routine report. The urge to publish is a result of the pressure on scientists to prove their ability to produce original ideas. The nearer to the frontiers of knowledge a scientist works, the greater is the pressure to succeed and the vulnerability of the individual to failure. The involvement of scientists with their peers is therefore a source of tension as well as of support.

Authors also write books from a viewpoint that is inevitably coloured by their own political ideology. An account by I. L. Horowitz of his reasons for writing *Revolution in Brazil* shows how the honest social scientist recognises this.[37] Horowitz was anxious to write a book about Brazil that did not contain the bias of many that had gone before. His own liberal view, transcending a purely nationalist perspective, led him to concentrate on areas of Brazilian life that had been of little interest before. But this was nevertheless a selection, honestly admitted to be a reflection of his own political views. A rare English example is Ford's expression of her socialism and hopes for an end to the system of stratification in Britain in her preface to her book *Social Class and the Comprehensive School*.[38]

The source of funds may also be an important influence on research. Sjoberg and many others have argued that major projects in American social science are prone to be influenced by the administration that sponsors the research, particularly where these sponsoring bodies are interested in maintaining social order. Thus

Project Camelot, lavishly supported by the US Army, was a study of the preconditions of internal conflict in Latin America and elsewhere. The social scientists had no apparent control over their work. Their critics have detected a stress on studying factors concerned with maintaining order so that the project seemed to some to be a study in counter-insurgency only.[39]

For most of human history thinkers who have supported unpopular views have been silenced by those in authority over intellectual life. The worst modern example occurred in Soviet Russia under Stalin. From 1929 bourgeois elements in science were under attack. In 1936 the Medico-Genetical Institute was attacked in *Pravda* and then closed. In 1937 Lysenko, with support from Stalin, branded his opponents as deviationists and his own theories replaced classical, Mendelian genetics. Leading opponents were arrested and Vavilov, the leading Russian geneticist, was arrested, sentenced to death and actually died in prison in 1942, the year he was elected to the Royal Society.

The final triumph of Lysenko came in 1948, when hundreds of scientists were dismissed from their posts, had their degrees removed, were shadowed by the secret police and arrested. Books were removed from libraries and all teaching of Mendelism banned. From 1948 to 1952 Lysenko was supreme in Russian biology.[40] He was the only scientist to be called great in his lifetime. At his first lecture at the Agricultural Academy, staff as well as students attended. A brass band played as he went to the rostrum. The State Chorus had a hymn honouring him.

During this period discoveries abounded. They became increasingly absurd, but the support of Stalin and then Khrushchev was sufficient to silence critics. However, from 1952 a counter-attack developed. At first it concentrated on detail without openly criticising Lysenko. But the damage done to Russian agriculture finally weakened Lysenko's grip on Soviet science until attempts were made to affect a compromise with classical genetics. By 1963 open attacks were appearing and the advances of Western biology could no longer be concealed. Khrushchev resigned in 1964 and Lysenko was dismissed in 1965.

The lessons of the Lysenko tragedy support the case for continuous scepticism in science as well as continuous replication to test claims. A combination of circumstances helped Lysenko attain power over more distinguished scientists. His claims seemed to offer practical solutions to Russia's problems in agriculture. He was able to align his theories with the current political ideology and obtain the support of Stalin and Khrushchev. By branding his opponents as deviationists, spies and saboteurs he clawed his way above them. In a centralised scientific community all training could be rapidly adjusted to the new doctrine.

Nevertheless, it was not just the ability of the secret police to silence opposition that accounted for this triumph of pseudo-science. Under the conditions in a dictatorship that maintained that its ideology was itself scientific, the sceptic was a heretic to be liquidated. The claim of the Russian leaders that Marxism as interpreted by them contained the key to all problems, including those tackled by scientists, meant there could be no dispute allowed with the official Party line. The grip was tightened by centralised control over all the possible means whereby critics could publicise their views. Furthermore, potential critics were isolated from the community of international scientists who might have supported them. It was not only biology that suffered from the political accusations of the Party leaders, but also the other natural sciences and all those subjects that study man which were flourishing elsewhere during this period.

The Lysenko case is an extreme example of the interference of government in science; similar, if less extreme, cases could be found in the witch-hunting during the McCarthy era in the United States in the first half of the 1950s. Once the direction of scientific activity is dictated from outside the scientific community, and once the allegiance of scientists is to governments, a source of scientific reliability is sacrificed. The drive of individual scientists to get the recognition of their fellows and the granting of this recognition only after agreement has been reached about evidence by established scientists may have undesirable effects, but does guarantee that fraud is unlikely to pass and that professional competence will be required before acceptance is accorded.

It is not only in totalitarian regimes that scientific activity has been controlled for political purposes. American and British scientists have lost their jobs because of their political beliefs. In 1970 there was a typical example of the suppression of a report attacking the established policies of a scientific community. A long discussion paper prepared by Huberman for Unesco was ordered to be destroyed by the Director General.[41] From surviving copies it is evident that this destruction was aimed to stop the circulation of a swingeing attack on the conventional policies of this agency and in education generally. Such book-burning has occurred periodically in history in a variety of different religious and political climates. Less obvious, but more general pressures come from colleagues, editors, censors and organisations providing the money for research. Furthermore, the public listens to, and buys, what it wants to hear and read. It is easy to pander to this self-satisfying taste and inhibit the distasteful and unpopular. The published is always selected.

Individual scientists are not only influenced by state policy and the views of agencies providing the money, but by their own personal ambition. Robert Hooke, a prolific inventor, was forever contesting with men like Newton and Huygens about who had invented things first. Cavendish, Watt and Lavoisier all claimed to have first demonstrated the compound nature of water. Sir Humphry Davy opposed the election of Michael Faraday to the Royal Society because he maintained that Faraday's discovery of electromagnetic rotation was not original.

A remarkable illustration of the mixture of personal ambition, determination to beat rivals and scientific inventiveness has been provided by Watson's account of his work with Crick on the structure of the D.N.A. molecule.[42] The book also demonstrates how an author unconsciously puts himself at the centre of events and of the creative process. The search for a model of this molecule that would satisfy existing knowledge was being sought in many places. Crick and Watson felt the pressure of competition as they neared their solution and feared that one of the other groups concerned would come up with a successful solution first. The discovery was seen as one which would qualify for a Nobel prize. While this account probably leaves out the more mundane work and the real expertise of those concerned, it is a startling revelation of the motivation of scientists working around the frontiers of knowledge.

The scientist is therefore under pressure to establish his prior claim. As a consequence it is usual in the journals of natural sciences to publish the date of receiving manuscripts. This is the case with most journals of psychology but unusual in sociology or education. The relation between originality and recognition also appears in the tendency to use the number of publications as a measure of accomplishment. The urge to publish and the recognition of genuine originality are part of the same tradition, though they may have little else in common.

There are rare instances where personal ambition seems to have led to fraud. The history of science is littered with deliberate deceptions and sincere fallacies, and the line between the two has often been difficult to draw. One of the most famous cases of this type was the discovery in 1911 of the Dawn Man of Piltdown by the amateur geologist and archaeologist Charles Dawson.[43] The support of Arthur Smith Woodward, a noted scientist, overcame most of the contemporary doubts about the reliability of the evidence. Although the remains did not fit in with other contemporary evidence and were to stay isolated phenomena the few doubters were not listened to. In 1913 digging and sieving exposed other remains and in 1915 Dawson found more remains of a second Piltdown man. The anticipated evidence of man's ape-like ancestry seemed to have been found. Dawson died in 1916 and no further remains were found. *Eoanthropus dawsoni* existed as an anomaly. By 1948 new techniques had showed that the Piltdown skull was not more than 50,000 years old. Next, parts of the skull were shown to be of different ages and constitution. Then staining was detected and the teeth were shown to have been filed down. The jaw was shown to be that of an orang utan. Implements found near the skull were shown to have been recently shaped and stained and most of the fossils found nearby were frauds. This was a forgery that had been the work of a professional, skilled enough to convince some of the most august scientists of the time. It may have been an elaborate joke, an attempt to obtain fame or a deliberate fraud. The important point is that such evidence had been expected and was sufficient to convince not only the public, but leading scientists of the time.

In both the natural and social sciences energy has been wasted. Great effort has gone into proving the obvious and probing the trivial. The commitment of scientists to their community can blind them to the futility of their work. But where the alchemist could waste little but his own time, moden scientific enterprises can absorb fortunes. Project Mohole seems to have started as a way of boosting the prestige of the earth sciences.[44] It was established as part of AMSOC, the American Miscellaneous Society, which had been founded as a comic contrast to established scientific societies. The object was to bore a hole deep into the earth's crust. But accurate costing, specific objectives and sound organisation were neglected amid professional envy and political chicanery. Estimates rocketed from 5 to 125 million dollars. In the end the project was stopped by Act of Congress in 1966. Significantly, this action followed articles in journals reporting science to the public in an intelligible way. Science, secure within communities, can easily obscure its shortcomings from the public.

CAN TEACHERS ACT PYGMALION IN THE CLASSROOM?

The history of education is strewn with simple solutions to complicated problems. But it is unlikely that a panacea for a many-sided symptom such as low attainment in school will suddenly be discovered. It is far more likely that the steady accumulation of evidence on the effectiveness of different methods of teaching, or approaches to individual children will affect improvement, than the discovery of a more potent style overnight. There is a lot of evidence to suggest that the self-image of a child is an important factor in determining achievement. But the nature of that image, the psychological and environmental factors that affect it, and the limits within which it can determine attainments are only slowly being uncovered. Yet in 1968, Rosenthal and Jacobson published *Pygmalion in the Classroom*,[1] describing an experiment in which teacher's expectations of children's performance were shown to bring that performance up to the expectations.

Rosenthal was a social psychologist who had an established reputation for his work on experimenter effects. This work at Harvard established a new field for psychological research. Jacobson was a school administrator. The book was hailed as a revelation in the popular press.[2] It remains one of the most widely quoted books on education, and Pygmalion effects became the basis of much pedagogical work in teacher training. But the psychologists who reviewed the book were mainly critical.[3] It seemed out-of-line with other work and the experimental design looked sloppy. Once Rosenthal and Jacobson had provided their data for reanalysis, and their methods were scrutinised, a thorough demolition was published, confirming the doubts of earlier reviewers.[4] Work on the effects of expectations continues, but this episode on *Pygmalion in the Classroom* is a reason for caution and scepticism.

The reviews of *Pygmalion in the Classroom* by psychologists focused on reliability. In particular Thorndike pointed out that the gains only applied to nineteen of the children and that for the rest gains were small, or that there was a deterioration following higher expectations.[5] Indeed, more children deteriorated than gained. But Thorndike, like other reviewers, was most concerned with the test used and the way results were analysed. To him, the data was so untrustworthy that any conclusions had to be suspect. Other reviewers pointed out that the teachers involved did not seem to have taken the experiment very seriously.[6] They may not have bothered to play their Pygmalion role. In natural experiments and intervention programmes it is assumed that the programme has been implemented. But later evaluations are often of the impact of resources applied for other than the intended purposes, or new methods that were never actually implemented.

The value of the Rosenthal and Jacobson study as a controversy comes from their release of their data to other researchers. Under the auspices of the National Society for the Study of Education, Elashoff and Snow published *Pygmalion Reconsidered* in 1971.[7] This reanalyses of the data, brings together reviews and other related work and contains a defence by Rosenthal and Jacobsen. But the conclusions of Elashoff and Snow are an indictment. Text and tables were seen as inconsistent, conclusions were over-dramatised, variables were misleadingly labelled and the findings were over-generalised.

The reviews of related work show that nine direct attempts to replicate Rosenthal and Jacobson's work failed.[8] The remaining work suggests that there is a relation between expectations and performance, but it is limited in scope and requires more than superficial attempts to modify the way teachers treat children. The work continues, but in spite of *Pygmalion in the Classroom*, rather than being boosted by it. Indeed, public confidence in psychological research could have been undermined by this episode, and the beneficial effects of getting teachers to raise their expectations of children thrown out with the discredited book. But few read the *American Educational Research Journal* or other professional publications where the criticisms were voiced, and Rosenthal and

Jacobson's work remains on the menu in teacher education and in the folklore of teaching.

There is however one aspect of the many criticisms that was rarely included in early criticisms, yet limits the generalisability of the work. Rosenthal and Jacobson are not clear in the book on the way the experimental and control groups were formed. As the groups were small and the children within them very varied, it was essential that the experimental and control groups were comparable on as many factors as possible in order to ensure that any differences that did emerge during the experiment were due to the expectations of teachers, and not to some other extraneous factors. The inferences drawn from the data, and the degree of generalisation, depend on this control over the sampling. Yet Rosenthal and Jacobson deliberately allowed the numbers of 'bloomers' in classes to vary from one to nine in classes that varied from sixteen to twenty-seven. Even more serious, while 478 children were given the pre-test, only 384 were given the post-test. It was impossible to see whether experimental and control groups lost comparable children, but for those who were tested before and after the experiment, those in the experimental group were higher in measured I.Q. Children with higher I.Q.s to begin with may have gained more. 'May have' because there is no way of knowing. But that also throws doubt on the inferences drawn from the differences between those exposed to high expectations and those who acted as controls, and makes it impossible to generalise the results. The samples drawn determine the conclusions and the extent to which generalisation is possible.

4

SAMPLING

The object of research is usually to generalise about the human condition. Information has to be collected from studies of specific groups which are available and, if possible, representative. Sampling has become the systematic way of choosing a group that is small enough for convenient data collection and large enough to be representative of the population from which it has been selected.

The representativeness of samples

There is a continual temptation to generalise from inadequate and irrelevant samples. Most social scientists are delivered from this temptation by the constraints exercised by the communities to which they belong. This is why writing a popular book or article involves a risk of loss of prestige among peers. But there are many writers who popularise social science from outside the discipline, free to generalise beyond limits that would be acceptable within academic life. In cutting through the mystery with which scientists surround themselves the populariser escapes the discipline as well.

Overgeneralisation is often not the original researcher's fault. Thomas, looking back over twenty years at the influence of his work on *The Polish Peasant*, confessed that he had developed an aversion to it because the methods and the data had been forgotten while certain theoretical conclusions for which there had originally been little foundation in the data remained popular and were reproduced regularly by other writers.[1] The original generalisation may have gone too far, but once the author's cautions had been pruned there was no limit to the generalisations of others.

It may be difficult to define a population to be studied. Old people or adolescents are not contained in single lists and arbitrary selection has to be made from incomplete sources such as cooperative general practitioners. Criminals are sampled from prison or court records. But in these and other cases there is no exact definition of the population from which a sample can be drawn. If you do not know in advance who are included as 'men in the street', it is questionable whether you can ever sample them in a representative way.

At worst a writer's views may be serving as a one-man sample. In other cases convenience or availability may have determined the sample. Unless the method of sampling is spelled out, scepticism is advisable. Students from one university department of psychology are unlikely to represent all students, all young persons or the human race. Monkeys caged in a zoo are unlikely to provide pertinent evidence for the explanation of normal human behaviour. Asylums, concentration camps and factories are often used to generalise about the organisation of schools, but it is worth remembering the differences between model and reality. However reliable the methods used in sampling, the group selected may only be representative of the specific population from which it was chosen.

This need to consider the representativeness of samples applies in all subjects. The historian has to be wary of generalising about a past population from evidence left by the rich who could afford to build to last and could leave written records. Anthropologists often observed the unusual rather than the normal and by the time observational techniques had improved, most of the small-scale societies had been colonised or fought over in the Second World War. The criminologist relied on criminals who had been caught rather than those successful in getting away with crime. In all subjects the most certain way of ensuring that a work is published is to concentrate on the problems and the deviations. This is legitimate provided these are not taken as a sample of the whole population.

There are two forms of sample used in the social sciences. The judgement, purposive or quota samples are all variations on the method of selecting individuals or groups who are seen to be representative of the target population. The judgement is that of the researcher, choosing what seems to him typical, relevant or interesting. It is purposive because the choice serves the objectives of the investigation. The quota sample allows the actual collector of information to use discretion in the final choice. The probability sample by contrast is selected as far as possible to eliminate the judgement or bias of the investigator. These are sometimes called random samples because at its most refined each member of the population is given an equal chance of selection. However, lucky dips are seldom used. It is more common to take a systematic sample from a list of names. Electoral registers, doctors' lists and record cards can be used to draw every nth name according to the total size of sample required.

Random samples do not guarantee representativeness. It is bad, but random luck, to draw a sample of all millionaires in a study of income distribution. It is small consolation that from a random sample the chances of this producing the results found can be calculated. Large samples reduce this kind of mischance, but are expensive. Only the Census draws a 100 per cent or a 10 per cent sample of the whole population.

The more usual procedure to ensure representation without excessive size is through stratification. This consists of breaking the population down into smaller homogeneous groups before sampling. A box of a hundred marbles, ten of ten different colours, could be sampled adequately by choosing one from each of the ten colours after they had been separated. To sample them and ensure representation without this stratification would take a much larger sample than ten. Stratification reduces the chance of fluke samples and enables the proportions in each strata to be fixed in advance. Hence most random samples ensure not an even chance of selection, but a known chance.

Judgement and probability samples are often combined. Thus a school or a factory may be selected first because it is convenient for the researcher. Then a random sample is taken within. For the reader this combination is important. The initial choice may have introduced bias which can be concealed under the mathematical calculations based on the second, random sampling. The examples that follow have been chosen because the methods of sampling are discussed by the authors. The reader is given a fair chance. They are amongst the most reliable. The most suspicious are those accounts which contain no description of sampling method. Here the third key question should be used, for the original sample determines the extent to which generalisations can be made.

Probability sampling

An accessible, typical and fully described probability sample can be found in the enquiry into young school leavers carried out by the Government Social Survey for the Schools Council.[2] Here teachers, parents, thirteen- to sixteen-year-olds and nineteen- and twenty-year-olds were interviewed to get the information useful for planning the raising of the school leaving age. This was a multi-stage sample, consisting of a first stage when 150 schools were sampled and then another stage when pupils, teachers and parents attached to these schools were selected.

The chances of the school being selected was determined by the number of school leavers in it. As 58 per cent of school leavers were in modern schools, 87 such schools were selected (58 per cent of 150). This method of allocating schools was continued for grammar and comprehensive schools. Then schools within each region were selected on the basis of the numbers in this age group within them. Thus 6.2 per cent of school leavers were in Wales so 5 of the 87 modern schools were picked from Wales (6.2 per cent of 87) and so on. Schools were then weighted according to the numbers of school leavers they contained and a random sample drawn from each region.

The second stage was to sample pupils and ex-pupils within the selected schools. This was done systematically from school registers, reducing the chance of bias by giving each school a random number at which to start the selection of names. In the end, 99 per cent of teachers, 94 per cent of parents, 96 per cent of thirteen- to sixteen-year-olds and 71 per cent of nineteen- and twenty-year-olds were interviewed. This is a base line against which other probability samples can be gauged. But the care taken was expensive, the spread of schools wide and the interviewing programme extensive. Few studies can afford to be so thorough.

Purposive sampling

Goldthorpe *et al.*, in their study of the affluent worker, had no lists available from which a probability sample could be taken.[3] To work within a budget they chose Luton as a likely town because of its prosperity, rapid growth, isolation from other traditional industrial areas, high proportion living on private housing estates and firms known for their high wages, advanced personnel and welfare services and good records of industrial relations.

This is typical of the better design of purposive sample. It focuses on a particular type of worker and a particular industrial situation. Working within a small budget it was impossible to spread the interviews to other areas or to sample all workers in a particular and high income group even if this was a practical possibility. In the event, Vauxhall Motors, Skefko Ball Bearing and Laporte Chemicals were selected within Luton. These employed 30 per cent of the town's labour force. Within these firms male employees between twenty-one and forty-six, married and living with their wives, resident in Luton, earning over £17 per week gross (in October 1962) and doing jobs central to the main production systems were to be the centre of the investigation. Within each firm, therefore, certain types of worker were selected by concentrating on a limited number of departments. This was necessary because it was time-consuming to get to know how each department worked, to get the management to agree to let more than a few departments be investigated, and to get the managers, supervisors and union officials in each department to agree to the interviewing programme. Within each department the aim was to interview all men who came within the interests of the study. Only in two of the larger departments within Vauxhall Motors was a sampling of individuals necessary. This was done at random from personnel records and was the only actual random sampling. This is not therefore a random sample, but the authors argue that it is nevertheless representative of the more affluent worker. The final sample of 326 individuals was selected to investigate a hypothesis, not for a descriptive survey. Representativeness was not the primary concern of the authors and they are careful not to generalise from it to the total population of affluent workers.

Purposive sampling is very common in the social sciences and education. It is necessary to get as much information as possible about the reasons for the choice of institution or group and for any peculiarities about them. It is good practice to ask why Floud, Halsey and Martin chose South-west Hertfordshire and Middlesborough for their important study of the relation between social class and educational opportunity.[4] Similarly the question should be asked of Jackson and Marsden's study of a Huddersfield grammar school,[5] Hargreaves of Lumley Secondary Modern,[6] Wakeford on public schools[7] and the choice of areas like Bethnal Green or Woodford[8] for community studies. In some cases it is convenience that determined choice. Thus the author made a seven-year follow-up study of a college of education in which he worked because this was convenient.[9] But this has dangers, for it was an arbitrary choice and meant that complete objectivity was difficult. Again, while each article on this particular work was carefully concluded by pointing out that generalisation was impossible because of the unique character of this college, this was rapidly forgotten as the evidence was used by later writers to illustrate general points about the training of teachers. Similarly Wakeford studied the public school where he went as a pupil, had a brother attending, was a member of the old boys' association and to which he returned as a temporary assistant master to act as participant observer to collect the information for the book.[10]

Thus a look at the way the sample was chosen should be followed by a continuing lookout for generalisation from limited cases. Affluent workers, juvenile thieves, working wives, new methods of teaching children to read are studied for their topical importance. But a sample chosen for convenience, because access is easy or because the school or area has some unique characteristic limits the study as a basis for generalisation. Psychologists often use students, especially psychology students, and generalise the results to the population as a whole. Delinquents are chosen from court records or penal institutions and used to reflect on all criminals, where they may be only representative of those that get caught. Schools where the headmaster is keen to let a researcher in are not typical, while those who are buzzing with innovations are exceptional and often welcoming. Patients of psychoanalysts, pupils at progressive schools, at small experimental schools like Malting House under a teacher of Susan Isaacs' ability,[11] schools carrying out new work that attracts ambitious staff and resources from curriculum development projects, can be very misleading bases for describing the general situation. Even worse, many are prepared to discuss human behaviour on the basis of observations of rats, monkeys and other animals. Even where these observations are in the natural habitat and not by the researcher on caged animals under experimental conditions, scepticism is the safest attitude. Random samples of a population may or may not be representative. But at least this depends on chance. Where the sampling is purposive there is not even a guarantee of an even chance unless the author takes the trouble to discuss his reasons for assuming his sample is representative.

The term 'quota sampling' is often applied to the type of sampling used in market research and opinion polling. In quota sampling, the interviewer is given a list with the types of person to contact. These are usually defined by such criteria as social class, age and sex. The interviewer gets a list with the numbers she is to contact of each type. She goes, for example, to areas where the twelve working-class married women workers between twenty and thirty years old that make up one quota are liable to be found. Then there is a search for a specified number with these characteristics previously defined in the office. In practice quota sampling gives reliable results with experienced interviewers, but because it is not random, is not open to mathematical procedures that can give a level of confidence in the results obtained. The speed, cheapness and absence of problems of finding particular individuals make quota sampling useful, but it lacks the mathematical basis that can indicate the chances of the results from a random sample being due to the particular sample that has been used.

Quota sampling depends on the judgement of the investigator. The interviewer tempted to fill her quotas with the alert woman with one child rather than tackling a harried mother of four, although the latter really fits the quota definition, is in the same position as the research worker tempted to use school X instead of Y because the former is welcoming and convenient. In both personal bias is entering before information has been collected and the outcome may be tinged by this subjective element.

In some cases quota sampling has to be used because it is impossible to find lists from which a probability sample of a population can be drawn. Thus there is no way of listing affluent workers or children of very high ability. They can only be sampled by choosing likely firms or schools and contacting those that fall within the definition of this particular population. The alternative is to take a very large probability sample and analyse separately those that fall into the appropriate categories.

One particularly hazardous form of purposive sampling is in the use of volunteers. Regardless of the safeguards that are built in, the reader is right to suspect that there is something unusual about those who step forward when a researcher asks for help. The most famous example of this is the Kinsey Report on human sexual behaviour.[12] Kinsey was determined to get a large sample and organised a campaign to interest clubs, families and other groups to volunteer. His object was to get 100 per cent samples from a number of different groups. However, while his final sample numbered 12,000, a minority were completed groups. Kinsey was aware of the dangers of volunteers and built in cross-checking techniques to detect distortions. This was a reason for wanting complete families or groups, for the answers could then be checked against others in the group.

The first volunteers were found to include many who were active, aggressive and exhibitionist. Kinsey tried therefore to obtain more reluctant volunteers by his recruiting campaign. He appealed for volunteers in the name of science, tried to establish advanced rapport in communities and to establish a reputation for scrupulous anonymity. But the suspicion remains that in such an intimate enquiry, those who come forward for interview are also those who are advanced in their behaviour. Furthermore, some groups such as homosexuals may be very reluctant to volunteer for fear of blackmail or prosecution, however secure the information was actually kept.

Dependence on volunteers is rare, but often someone in authority or position of influence may provide the volunteers. Thus Veness, in her study of school leavers, first got permission from the education officers of a county and then invited headteachers to volunteer their schools for investigation.[13] Similarly Phillips got information on small social groups in England from friends willing to help.[14] Work relying on such samples must be read as illustrations of the attitudes and behaviour of those who are cooperative or are not in a position to say no. Similarly, samples from those attending clubs, those at home during the day or using public libraries are not likely to be typical. A study such as Hemming's *Problems of Adolescent Girls*, based on 3,259 letters to a weekly journal between April 1953 and March 1955, is representative only of girls who write about their problems to magazine 'aunties'.[15] The greatest blunder in survey history was the 1936 Literary Digest poll, predicting that Landon would defeat Roosevelt, on the basis of a postal questionnaire from a sample drawn from the telephone directory, thus eliminating many poorer voters.[16]

There is no simple way of assessing whether a sample is adequate. Three important features of sampling have to be considered. First, as long as sampling is being used it is a matter of how much chance there is of freak samples being drawn, never a matter of certainty. This is why results from random sampling are expressed in terms of probability or levels of confidence. Second, the larger the sample, the more confidence there can be that a freak selection will not be made. Thirdly, the greater the variety of the characteristics in the population being measured the larger the sample needs to be. One tin soldier from thousands from the same run of production suffices as a test of quality. But the physical features of humans and even more their behaviour and attitudes are very varied and a larger sample is needed. The greater the spread of the feature being measured around the mean, the larger the sample size has to be. This is why stratification is commonly used, for it arranges the population into groups so that each contains persons of similar age, class, education and so on, thus reducing the necessary sample size. The confidence that can be placed in the adequacy of a sample therefore varies inversely with the distribution of the characteristics being measured and directly with the numbers in the sample.

Response

The care with which a sample has been designed will be wasted if those chosen cannot be found or refuse to cooperate. The response rate is probably the most important single indicator of the reliability of a survey. The reader should try to find evidence that response has been considered as a design problem, that there were efforts to minimise non-response and that there was some attempt to investigate the character of the non-responders. Finally, the frankness with which the author discusses the response issue can be taken as an index of his concern to give the reader the chance to assess the dependability of the work.

The following are samples of response rates in different types of survey.

Postal questionnaires

J. GABRIEL, *The Emotional Problems of the Teacher in the Classroom*,[17] response rate to first questionnaire to individual teachers, 35 per cent, second questionnaire, 29 per cent.

F. MUSGROVE, *Youth and the Social Order*.[18] Questionnaire to adults in towns, response rate, 32 per cent, in suburbs, 34 per cent.

Surveys using interviews

J. and E. NEWSON, *Infant Care in an Urban Community*.[19] Response rate 92 per cent, including 1.6 per cent refusals.

P. WILLMOTT, *Adolescent Boys of East London*.[20] Response rate 88 per cent, including 8 per cent refusals.

Follow up studies

J.W.B. DOUGLAS, *The Home and the School*,[21] contained full information from 5,418 from sample first drawn in 1946. In 1948, 4,742 completed interviews and in 1950, 4,668. During the first four years of the children's lives, 4.3 per cent died and 4.5 per cent emigrated. By the time of the Home and the School survey, 4.9 per cent had died and 6.7 per cent had emigrated.

F.W. MILLER and others, *Growing up in Newcastle upon Tyne*,[22] studied 847 five-year-olds but of the 1,142 children born between 1 May and 30 June 1947; 49 had died, 239 moved away and 7 left the survey by 1952.

These figures bring out important points about the design of surveys. First, postal questionnaires usually get very low response. Second, well organised interview programmers can obtain around a 90 per cent response. The Government Social Survey usually attains this figure. Third, follow-up studies suffer from great difficulties in tracing the original sample.

The importance of looking carefully at the proportion not responding lies in the possibility that they are not a random sample and may not be similar to those who respond. The interview technique has the advantage that the refusals can be assessed. But in the postal questionnaire, there is no way of knowing whether those who did not reply forgot, were too scared to answer or rugged individualists who would have liked to have told the sender to get lost. There is always the suspicion that the non-responders may have been the most interesting and certainly the most non-conformist group. Thus an attempt in the Authoritarian Personality study to use mailed questionnaires was abandoned, not only because only 20 per cent responded, but because those that did reply were found to be biased in a democratic direction.[23]

Non-response also makes it difficult to interpret generalisations. If 100 out of 200 respond and 90 of these answer YES, does this mean that 90 per cent are in favour or 45 per cent? There is no way of really knowing, although the assumption is usually that those who replied are representative and a huge majority are in favour. But the half who did not reply may have been so violently opposed that they tore up the questionnaire and threw it in the fire.

It is therefore important to look for attempts to anticipate and reduce non-response. Calling back on those who were not in when the interviewer called usually finds a few more. The Government Social Survey insists that it is the duty of an interviewer to call at any time, however inconvenient, or to fix an appointment for a later period to get near a complete response. Even where refusal or failure to contact is finally accepted, there should have been some attempt to assess the characteristics of non-responders. Similarly a follow-up letter with another stamped addressed envelope can bring in more completed forms from a postal questionnaire.

These additions to those responding are not only important in themselves, but can be used to see whether those who cannot be contacted at first or do not reply differ in any systematic way from those responding at first. This is the only way of estimating whether non-responders differ from responders. Thus if it is found that half the people who cannot be contacted in a survey are young married couples, this proportion can be used if it has been decided to bring the number up to that originally intended by additions after failure to contact.

Finally, it must be remembered that non-response occurs only in probability sampling. In purposive samples contacts are made until a quota is filled. The advantages of probability samples are in providing a reliable basis for generalisation and for mathematical calculations. But very often non-response makes a mockery of any complex statistical calculations. It is the way statistics can lend an aura of competence to inadequate samples that makes it essential to find response rates. Studies have been discussed here because they contained these rates. None are therefore as suspect as those in which non-response rates have been omitted.

CONTROVERSY 5

HAVE WE UNDERESTIMATED THE REASONING POWER OF YOUNG CHILDREN?

Jean Piaget is an intellectual giant. He has researched into, and written about, the development of human cognition for over fifty years. This work was aimed at producing a model of psychological development grounded in biology and illuminated by philosophy. Out of this work one small segment, the theory that human development proceeds through stages, has been influential within education, although Piaget has showed little interest in classroom practices. Its utilisation as a guide to practice in the Plowden Report on English primary schooling, not only when child development was discussed, but when recommendations were made about curriculum and teaching methods is typical.[1] Yet research already published in the late 1960s suggested that Piaget's work was flawed, and more recent research has confirmed this.[2] We may not only have underestimated the reasoning capacity of young children, but, as a consequence, may have handicapped those children by adopting restricted teaching methods.

This Controversy links chapters on data collection to those on the presentation and interpretation of evidence. It is concerned with the use made of Piaget's work, rather than the work itself. But it is not only that experimental work is now producing a different picture of human cognitive development, but that there is now doubt about the usefulness of the model for educators. Indeed, Piaget's own more recent work has been away from stage theory and towards historical and comparative methods. But textbooks in education abound with references to stage theory, and generations of primary school teachers have been prepared to adjust their teaching in line with Piaget's model of development built around stages.

Donaldson has used recent research, testing some of Piaget's theories to demolish the idea that children under six or seven are egocentric, incapable of perceiving events from any but their own veiwpoint.[3] Piaget's experiments with young children may not have made sense to the children. When the problem set was similar, asking them to perceive a situation from the viewpoint of others, but the task familiar to them, researchers have found that another point of view was taken. The nature of the experiment, not the capacity of the child, may have determined the results.

This is not merely of theoretical interest. Donaldson's book details the practical implications of accepting the ability of young children to decentre, and the adverse consequences of the belief that they could not. The notion that there was a stage below which children were egocentric also meant that they were not seen as capable of deductive reasoning until they were six or seven. Again this was based on experimental work that was replicated and applied to the teaching of subjects such as mathematics.[4] Yet Donaldson reports many experiments setting the same tasks but in ways that made sense to the children where they could infer from one set of conditions to another by abstract thought of the 'if A is greater than B, and B is greater than C, then A must be greater than C' type. Here one early repeat of Piaget's experiment using an altered design will be used to illustrate what happens when a cornerstone of education is chipped away.

In 1971, Bryant and Trabasso reported that their experimental work showed that young children could make transitive inferences, thus refuting Piaget's conclusions.[5] Following hard on the publication of the Plowden Report and on the publication of many books that assumed the reliability of Piaget's work it was bound to be news. The press seized on the Bryant and Trabasso replications and headlines in *The Observer* of 'Children scupper Piaget's Law' were followed elsewhere by reports of Piaget's theory being undermined and by forecasts of major changes in teaching methods.[6] The *Daily Telegraph*, after reporting that the educational world would never be the same again, went on to predict that primary school teachers could now get down to teaching rather than minding fun parties.[7] These reports, in line with the political leanings of the papers concerned, turned out to be based on a telephone call from an *Observer* reporter to Bryant.[8] Inevitably there was dispute over what he actually said and when he complained that he had been misinterpreted.

There is little doubt that the popular version of undermining and scuppering will pass into educational folklore. The *Observer* article that sparked off the controversy appeared on 22 August 1971. The Byrant and Trabasso article had appeared on 13 August 1971, but in *Nature*, a journal not usually read by those interested in discussing education.

By the end of the 1970s the over-simplification in the *Either We're Too Early and They Can't Learn It or We're Too Late and They Know It Already* dilemma that stopped most attempts to apply Piaget had been recognised in the journals, although in few popular books.[9] Experimental curricula having aims derived from Piaget's developmental stages had only served to expose the ambiguities in stage theory itself. The evidence seems to point to a choice between a curriculum that emphasises the learning of basic skills at the expense of intellectual curiosity, and another that stresses independent learning at the cost of reading and numerical skills. Following what was assumed to be Piagetian principles into classroom action has led to the dilemma italicised above.

There is a worrying question over this Controversy. To any sceptic, Piaget's stages seemed arbitrary and often a violation of common sense. It seemed obvious that young children were doing things spontaneously that infant school teachers said were impossible at such an early age. The answer to this rather tragic situation, which must have penalised generations of children, probably arose because of the many stages between the original work and its translation and extension into practical advice. Piaget's research as a biologist started in 1911 and his work on the mollusk is still referred to by him in books published in the late 1970s. There was little interest in the English-speaking world until the 1950s. Thus many books have been translated long after original publication. But that translation has not been easy, for the original style is dense and tightly constructed. One writer has likened Piaget's work to the Bible in its capacity for conflicting interpretation.[10]

A multi-level Piaget industry has grown. First there are Piaget's own originals. Then come translations into English. Then there are texts for students of psychology, some close to the original, some simplifications. Then there are many 'Piaget for Teachers' texts written in a simple but inevitably simplified style. Finally there are attempts to produce practical suggestions for teaching parts of the curriculum, based on Piagetian principles. The sequence is translation, interpretation, simplification and operationalisation. Something is very likely to get lost on the way. Any report that Piaget's Law has been scuppered is liable to be a reference to something that he never formulated and, if related to education, something in which he would have little interest. Piaget has been used to justify particular classroom practices. But this has never been the focus of his work. The evidence produced by original thinkers is often presented and interpreted in ways that are alien to them.

5

STUDIES BASED ON OBSERVATION

All research depends on observation. Through the ears and eyes the material and social world is interpreted. But this perception is not passive. Impressions are first selected and then interpreted within the mind of the observer. Between the impression on the senses and the reported interpretation are the attitudes, values and prejudices, as well as the academic conceptual models, of the researcher. Perception is the process of fitting what is seen or heard into these maps and frameworks in the mind.

A psychologist may see a classroom as a situation of organised learning experiences reinforcing correct and inhibiting incorrect answers. A sociologist may see the same scene as a group constrained by the power of the teachers and the interaction of peers. A teacher may see it as a situation to be controlled, a parent as a group affecting their child, a head teacher as a reflection on the competence of the teacher and an inspector as a guide to the efficiency of the school. Individuals enter situations with maps already established in their minds into which they fit the evidence of their senses.

The effect of cultural differences on observation can be gauged from the improbable but delightful contrast between German and American psychologists observing hungry rats confronted by a maze in which food was available at the far end. Both sets of rats learned to traverse the maze. But those seen by the Germans sat pondering the problem in an immobile way until a solution dawned and they threaded their way through. American rats, however, launched themselves hell for leather in a series of bruising trial runs until they learned from their errors. The time taken was similar, the style contrasting. Any student who has puzzled over the differences between gestalt and behaviourist theories of learning will realise that this ludicrous picture reflects an underlying discrepancy due to national differences which seem to have established different frames of reference in the minds of the two national groups which developed these theories.

A more serious if still amusing example of the effects of the expectations of the observer can be demonstrated by Rosenthal and Fode's experiment with twelve psychology students asked to measure the time taken for rats to learn to run to the darker arm of a maze to find food.[1] Sixty ordinary rats were divided between the students, but six students were told they had maze-bright rats and six were given maze-dull rats, each sample said to be specially bred. Each rat was given ten chances each day for five days to learn that the darker arm led to food.

While there was no actual difference in the maze-learning ability of the rats, the students observed the results that they were led to anticipate by the description of their sample as bright or dull. The bright rats not only became better performers but showed daily improvement, while the dull rats only improved to the third day and then deteriorated. Furthermore, the dull rats refused to start at all more frequently than the eager-to-get-with-it bright ones and were slower to reach the end after they had learned. After the experiment was over the students rated their rats and their own attitudes towards them. Those having 'bright' rats viewed them as brighter, more pleasant and more likeable, and their own attitude towards the rats was more relaxed and enthusiastic than among the six students with the 'dull' sample.

Such effects are not confined to the social sciences, although the frequent use of human beings as subjects of research makes them more prone to self-fulfilling effects. In the natural sciences a researcher can be similarly misled, either by the expectations of colleagues or his own predictions and hopes. Once set to expect a result, a scientist in all fields is liable to find his observations biased. This is why controls and repetitions of experiments by others are so important. In the natural sciences the use of measuring instruments eliminates much of the dependence on human perception, but bias still occurs. This is the central paradox of science.

In 1903 Blondlot announced the discovery of n-rays, which gave no photographic effect but could be detected through observing their effect on the luminosity of phosphorescent surfaces. The discovery was quickly confirmed by other French scientists, and by 1904, seventy-seven scientific publications had included descriptions of the applications of these rays, how to detect them, the materials that emitted them, their wavelength and spectrum. Yet outside France no one seemed to be able to detect *n*-rays through replicating Blondlot's work. In 1904, shortly after Blondlot had been awarded the Lalande prize for his discovery, the rays were shown to be the result of his faulty observations. The discovery of X-rays by Rontgen in 1896 had led to a great interest in such phenomena, and Blondlot and others were too ready to be convinced by their own fallible perception. After 1909 the *n*-ray passed out of science, its discoverer having gone mad. Poor Professor Rene or Prosper or plain M Blondlot, Blondot or Blandot: even in death he is not respected, for these three versions of his name appeared in the three references cited here.[2]

This long introduction has been necessary, not only because information is collected through observation alone, but because observation is a part of every research technique. Humans involved in investigating have to try to control the factors that could bias their own perceptions. This is not easy, for most of these influences have been learned and are tied up with personal hopes, fears, ambitions and needs. The investigator is always a factor in the experimental situation.

Once again the social scientist faces a unique difficulty. Most observation is also interaction. The researcher is also being observed. His presence will disturb the natural scene. The behaviour he sees may be a response to his presence.

The control of observation

In the history of science it is often difficult to sort out fiction from the genuine scientific theory. Science has always been mixed up with religion and mysticism. Astrology and alchemy contained astronomy and chemistry. Men practised 'mysteries', sought the Philosopher's Stone, elixirs and magic numbers. As they did so scientific techniques were developed. A man like Leonardo da

Vinci was artist, visionary and scientist. Teilhard de Chardin in the twentieth century similarly mixed imagination with scientific fact. Science has drawn inspiration from the artist and the scientist has inspired the artist.

The social sciences are similarly rooted in traditions where imagination and observation are fused. Many books are based on imagination or casual memories. Others draw on the memories of others and trust that the questions asked got valid replies. Others are just the opinions of the author. Yet all may be classified as social science and be written in the customary, convincing style. Libraries are graveyards testifying to the fallibility of armchair theorising of this kind. Books remain on shelves to confuse the living.

The pollution of interpretation with personal interests, values and memories make it important to look for controls over reported observations. Again, it is the casual observation or those studies where no actual techniques are reported that are suspect. Only those studies careful enough to give the reader sufficient information can be criticised.

The first set of controls exists within subject disciplines. An anthropologist in a tribal community, a psychologist peering at children through a one-way mirror or a sociologist lurking round a crowd at a football match are, in part at least, controlled by the discipline they practise and have learned. The observations are fitted into specific subject frameworks and there converted into anthropological, psychological or sociological facts, open to criticism by colleagues.

Studies can also be controlled through preliminary fixing of the conditions under which observation is to be made. This can consist of controls over what is to be looked at, how and when it is to be viewed or how the information is to be recorded. The aim is to build in checks over the observer and to enable those that read or follow him to know exactly what was observed, to replicate and check the results. Teams of observers, timed observations, check lists, films and tape recordings have all been used to eliminate dependence on the unaided individual.

Reiss has argued that there is no necessary distinction between observational techniques and social surveying either in power to discover the new or in control over the research process.[3] He used carefully selected, trained and supervised observers to study crime and the work of the police in metropolitan areas. There were standardised procedures for recording events as they happened. The thirty-six observers, selected from over 200 who were interviewed for the job, were allocated to eight areas with high crime rates in each of three cities. In each city, days, police watches and beats were sampled. Every effort was made to detect and reduce errors in observing by regular supervision.

The degree of detachment

Observers can either participate in the activity they are observing, remain detached or, as is most usual, adopt some position in between. Only in those rare cases where one-way mirrors or some other screening device are used, or the observed are oblivious to the presence of an observer, are the subtle adjustments due to social interaction missing. These adjustments affect the behaviour of both observer and observed.

The decision over the degree of involvement in the activity to be observed is usually made after considering the possible distorting effect on the activity through the presence of an observer. A fully participant observer may fit in with the group so smoothly that it will go on behaving naturally. This is particularly the case where members of the group do not know that one or more of their number are observers gathering information. But even where the researcher is known to be after information, he may be accepted and little distortion may result.

Participant observation is valuable because it enables groups to be observed in an unforced situation. Its weakness comes from the same situation. The act of becoming involved threatens the maintenance of objectivity. Thus the reader should still be asking the basic questions, how reliable is this observation, how valid are the results? The results of participant observation may be valid because there has been no distortion of the situation, but reliability is doubtful. Another observer might see things very differently once he started to participate and observe.

This is, once again, the fundamental dilemma of social science. Involvement is necessary for understanding, but science is a detached activity. An American watching his first cricket match could soon explain the action by referring it to his previous experience. But only by getting among cricketers and preferably playing the game could he come to understand it and interpret it accurately. But this involvement would lead to affection, emotion replacing detached assessment. Western observers of simple societies face the same difficulty. So do observers of children, youth groups, gangs, dropouts and drug addicts.

Frankenberg sees participant observation as proceeding through an early stage of acclimatisation within the culture being studied, to an internalisation of that culture.[4] From this point the observer has learned a new perspective that he can draw on in addition to his own native view of the world. But a final stage has to be reached in order to communicate with an audience. At this point the involvement gives way again to objectivity. This sequence occurs in all social scientific research and illustrates the dilemma of balancing involvement and detachment. Stage one is liable to involve harsh judgements on the group being studied. Stage two is liable to involve a romantic, tolerant view and stage three will be marked by a return to objective, yet informed attitudes.

The effect of participating on the observer

The reflections of participant observers have dramatically illustrated the impact of involvement on the observer. Thus Gans, studying the American middle class in Leavittown, tried to remain the outsider but was subject to an internal tug-of-war as the community involved him.[5] The difficulty of gaining entry and acceptance, the urge to have someone to talk to about the work and the feeling that he was inevitably deceiving people increased the strain.

Gans has also suggested that field work attracts those who are in some way alienated from their own background. Participating and observing becomes therefore an educating process. This is illustrated in the three central essays of Vidich, Bensman and Stein's collection, *Reflections on Community Studies*.[6] Seeley, discussing his work in Crestwood Heights, contrasts theorising about society with actually entering a society.[7] The sociology he was taught seemed disembodied, a sophisticated, shared illusion.

This innocence was shattered when he got into the field. The neat theory was disintegrated by the reality. But the research also forced him to analyse the relation between his own childhood experience, his personality and his choice of profession.

Stein reflecting on his own prior analysis of community studies also detected a personal conviction, based on his experiences in the field, that the sociology he had learned and the techniques for collecting information that were recommended could not generate insight.[8] To participate and understand in a concrete situation meant first detaching oneself from the standards of professional sociology.

Wolff, who spent periods spread over twenty years studying a community in New Mexico, uses the word surrender to describe his experience.[9] He became totally involved and shelved theoretical ideas as he immersed himself in the community. Wolff, like Stein and Seeley, found the human situation too complex, too emotional, to match the neutral systems of sociological theory. All these writers had also to work out fresh methods of research suitable for a situation in which they were deeply involved and in which accepted methodology with its emphasis on objectivity was inadequate.

At the other extreme from the attempt to get accepted within the group to be studied is non-participant observation, in which the observer remains deliberately detached. This not only eliminates the chance of his perception of the situation being biased by his affection for the group and eliminates the chance of members feeding him with false information, but enables the maximum number of controls to be established over the observation. But there is an accompanying risk that lack of insight will result from lack of involvement. The meaning of events may be misunderstood.

The ethics of observation

In all observational studies there is an issue of confidence. The researcher is asking for cooperation or observing without explaining the situation to those observed. In the first case, the ethical question arises over what to publish, for those who have agreed to participate may object to published accounts of their behaviour. In the second case the observer is a voyeur and his report may have all the intimacy of a Peeping Tom's notebook, and all its legitimacy.

This issue is complicated by the dilemma that the scientist is in if he starts observing without the consent of the observed or by clandestine means. He is nevertheless a scientist committed to report what he finds and not to conceal information or distort it to protect his informants. This dilemma can be followed in the work of Whyte on street corner gangs.[10] Here it was a combination of respect for those who had befriended him and provided the information, coupled with a fear that adverse accounts of them would put the author in danger of being carved up. Whyte's study lasted four years. By the end he was playing an active part in Cornerville society. To his informants he was writing a book. He visited them after publication to gauge its impact. Perhaps this is an indication of the compromise nature of the book. Nevertheless it remains a classic, and its methodological appendix has a full discussion of the ethical issues.

A similar case was the study of a small town by Bensman and Vidich.[11] Here the presence of the social scientists was not realised by the inhabitants. Vidich has dicussed the dilemma of publication, but in this case the decision was to publish because scientific procedures took precedence over obligations to the town. The difficulty here is that all fictionally named towns, schools and organisations are soon known by name. To Bensman and Vidich this was a refusal to fix the data to avoid exposing the private lives of the citizens. It could be argued, however, that the original decision to gather information surreptitiously was itself unethical.

Probably the most fascinating but most morally dubious study was Festinger, Riecken and Schachter's *When Prophecy Fails*.[12] Here the authors and their students infiltrated a group who had prophesied that the end of the world was nigh. The social scientists were fully accepted and even after the world carried on passed its predicted end, another observer was introduced to check on the impact of this miscalculation on the group. Recording was done in the toilet, out on the porch or on midget tape recorders. This was an extreme example, but most social scientists have experienced moments when they have access to information that is obviously private. Publish and be damned can be justified on scientific grounds, but a public conned once is unlikely to cooperate again. Furthermore, social scientists are not exempt from the responsibility to exercise power over others with restraint.

Styles of observation

Observation can be rigidly controlled or be used so that the observed are not disturbed or even aware of the scrutiny. At one extreme are the studies of Bales.[13] Small groups, in specially designed rooms, were observed by specially trained observers sitting behind one-way mirrors. These observers were trained and tested until their observations were reliable. Predetermined categories of behaviour were used to complete schedules which were subject to standardised processing. The observers were checked against each other, against expert recorders and against their own previous performance. But the obvious criticism is that the situation was so artificial that the results have no significance for normal behaviour in small groups. The use of interaction scales in school classrooms can attain the same reliability but have the same suspect validity.

At the other extreme was Mass Observation.[14] This was a typical unobtrusive means of collecting information on normal behaviour on such days as the Coronation of King George V on 12 May 1937. Around 1,000 observers noted anything that interested them, details of overheard conversation, striking local events, the weather and the response of people to the event. Similar day-surveys have left a record of normal routines, contacts, feelings and impressions. The observers were a very articulate, and mildly radical group. There was no control over their observations. The accounts are still vivid but have all weaknesses of inductive methods. With no guidance from any hypothesis or definition of issue or population to be observed, there is little that could be a springboard for later work.

The attractions of participant observation are that the natural situations is preserved and the understanding can be deep. The technique has gained in popularity as social scientists have moved away from attempts to copy the methods of the natural sciences and towards interpreting the meaning given to events by those involved. This shift in methods is covered in Chapter 9. But participant observation involves more than just joining in the action and waiting for insights. Thus Becker has argued for a formalisation and systematisation of the method to reduce its artistic and increase its scientific content.[15] To Becker, participant observation should follow the steps that are conventional in any systematic research. Attention should be paid to the selection and definition of problems, concepts and indicators, to cross-checking the observations made and to referring the results to some theoretical model in order to come to conclusions.

Becker is arguing that participant observation can be a rigorous, reliable method. He has used it to look at the careers of dance band musicians, schoolteachers, marihuana users and medical students. These studies paint a picture of the world of the groups studied as seen by them. There is no doubt that getting involved in a group gives access to their way of making sense of the world, although it is the researcher's account that is in print. The act of involvement brings its problems. Even when there is continuing reference to available theory and continual cross-checking of the different sources of information, the very act of involvement is liable to increase the chances of bias.

It is not easy to illustrate bias in observational studies because replication is not easy. The group or its environment will have changed across time. The participation of a different observer may have its effect. Replication is in any case rare. However, in 1951, Oscar Lewis published his *Life in a Mexican Village: Tepoztlan Revisited*.[16] This was a study of communities previously studied by Redfield in the 1930s.[17] Redfield had seen Tepoztlan as a society in which there was little change, a strong sense of belonging together and a homogeneity among the inhabitants. Lewis, in re-studying the community, was not trying to prove Redfield wrong, but looking for the type of errors that could be made in community studies. To Lewis, Tepoztlan manifested individualism not cooperation, tensions, fear and distrust rather than Redfield's picture of contentment and a sense of community. Later, in 1969, Avila published another study of this area of Mexico and again refuted the view that change was slow or the people uncompetitive.[18]

It may be that the community had genuinely changed over the period from the 1930s to the 1950s and 1960s. But it may have been that Redfield saw information that fitted into the folk-urban continuum that was his theoretical model. The hypothesis may have directed the observations. Redfield later tried to explain the differences between himself and Lewis.[19] He points out that both he and Lewis would have brought their own views into their work, and would have been alerted to see activity that confirmed their very different positions on urban and rural life. Once again this is an illustration of the way 'facts' are created by reference to theory. Where the theories differ, so may the 'facts'.

Everything that has been written about observation in this chapter applies to those that follow. Natural as well as social scientists tend to observe what they expect. Because we have to refer what we see to some scientific or everyday model of events to convert it into a fact, perception is structured by anticipation. But that anticipation is affected not only by theoretical models, but by political or personal beliefs. These too are organised as models to which we refer the impressions on our senses. There may also be a connection between these models. Someone who holds a conflict model as appropriate for the social world is liable to see the conflict and feel it around him. Functionalists are more liable to see the persistence of human relations, and to feel the smooth working of human arrangements. Personal, professional and political views are liable to cohere and to influence observation. The reader needs to look behind the accounts of observational studies to the view of the world held by the author.

CONTROVERSY 6

DO THE PUBLIC WANT RELIGIOUS EDUCATION IN STATE SCHOOLS?

This controversy revolves around a simple question about the attitude of the public towards religious education in schools. That each party in the dispute can present evidence to support its own case is explicable in the light of the preceding chapters. But here another feature is significant. Two of the surveys involved were carried out by the same research agency. Yet the results still reflected the opposed views of the two bodies paying for the survey.

Every state school in England must hold a daily act of worship and give lessons in religious instruction. The controversy over these clauses in the Education Act of 1944 has been continuous in the history of state schooling. Outraged humanists battle with entrenched churchmen. In the middle the public seems to become increasingly apathetic. Given the confusing nature of the evidence the antagonists provide, this public apathy is fair criticism of what is claimed to be conclusive evidence.

Here two surveys supporting extreme views will be compared. Both were based on probability samples of around 2,000 persons. Both used interviewers asking apparently simple questions. Both were carried out by National Opinion Polls.

The survey commissioned by *New Society* and reported by Goldman in 1965 claimed that 90 per cent of the sample wanted the present arrangements to continue and for religious instruction in schools to remain unchanged in both primary and secondary schools.[1] The survey commissioned in 1969 by the British Humanist Association found that out of eight objectives of schooling, the sample ranked 'help in becoming a convinced Christian' and 'information about Christianity and other world religions' sixth and seventh for boys and sixth and fifth for girls over twelve years old.[2] The conclusion drawn here was that there was no real expression of support for the retention of religious instruction. Barring some dramatic change in public attitude in four years, the neutral conclusion is that in some no doubt honest way, the opinions of the sponsors had percolated into the research design.

The questions themselves give no obvious clue to the way this bias could have been introduced. The descriptions of the research are inadequate for any other part of the design to be examined thoroughly.

The *New Society* survey asked 'Should the present school religious arrangements continue?' and 'Do you want religious instruction as it is, or none?' Ninety per cent replied 'yes' and 'as it is'. The Humanist Association claimed that this was the equivalent of asking 'Do you like tea?' and taking the answer 'yes' to mean a dislike of coffee, as no alternative form of education was offered. Curiously, they chose the same research agency to do their own survey.

The 1969 British Humanist Association survey used show cards on which the key question was 'Which of the following do you think is most important in the education of schoolboys (schoolgirls) over the age of twelve years?' There followed a list of objectives in schooling. Only 4 per cent chose 'information about Christianity and other world religions' or 'help in becoming a convinced Christian' for boys and 5 per cent for girls. Given the obvious importance of the other objectives it could be argued that these questions were the equivalent of asking people to chose whether water or tea was more important for survival.

If extreme views seem to produce extreme answers to questions, do agencies having no strong views get compromise answers? The 1966 Schools Council Enquiry Number 1 (*Young School Leavers*) seems to suggest that they do.[3] This survey was only concerned to rank groups of subjects. The Government Social Survey asked, 'Do you think it is very important, fairly important or not important that (name of parent's child) should be taught (subjects) at school?' There were thirteen groups of subjects. Religious instruction was seen as very important for boys by 43 per cent of the sample and for girls by 45 per cent. For boys and girls alike religious instruction was ranked seventh out of the thirteen groups in the percentage seeing it as very important.

This conflicting evidence could only aggravate the existing confusion over the religious issue in English education. Not surprisingly the 1970 Durham Report on religious education referred to actual surveys of opinion on only one of its 577 pages and then only to gauge whether England was or was not a Christian country.[4] The efforts to survey public opinion were either ignored, not considered valuable or not known to the authors.

6

INFORMATION THROUGH ASKING QUESTIONS

If you want an answer, ask a question. Whether it is an attempt to reconstruct the past, describe the present or predict the future, the questionnaire and the interview have come to dominate the collection of information in the social sciences, particularly sociology. Yet, 'When did you last . . . ?', 'How many times did you . . . ?' and 'How will you . . . ?' are questions that will not just produce answers but will reconstruct the meaning of the situation in which the asker and answerer are involved. The asking of questions is the main source of social scientific information about everyday behaviour, yet between question and answer there may be shifts in the relation between scientist and subject. The final answers emerge from this interaction and the meanings that each party gives to the situation. The questions have created this situation and the answers are meaningful only in its context.

Asking questions to get valid answers is therefore a skilled and sensitive job requiring knowledge of the environment in which the questionnaire is to be filled in or the interview conducted. It requires knowledge of the likely impact of questioner on respondent. It requires a sensitivity to the symbolic sophistication of humans, non-verbal as well as verbal. Imagine, with Jowell and Hoinville, a poll conducted among coloured immigrants to discover their attitudes towards subsidised repatriation to their country of origin shortly after a speech by Enoch Powell.[1] Such a poll for Panorama by Opinion Research Centre asked such questions as 'Would you like to return to your country of origin if you received financial help?' Asked this way a majority might be expected to say 'yes'. But now imagine the question being asked by white, middle-class, middle-aged women interviewers, on a rainy, cold day in late November in the middle of the Black Country. To anyone even capable of envisaging Trinidad or Jamaica the answers 'Yes', 'No', or 'Don't know' are more likely to have meant 'Yes please', 'Get lost' or 'How much!' A thought about the interaction and shifting of ground that was likely to have occurred in those macabre interviews should say more than any interactionist treatise. Yet similar scenes must have been enacted in the accumulation of the evidence on race relations in Controversy 11.

There is a whole spectrum of situations in the use of questionnaires and interviews, ranging from the postal questionnaire where there is no direct contact, to the psychoanalyst's couch where there is much. The same problems are present as in observational studies, particularly those of the degree of control and the amount of interaction. The postal questionnaire is not exempt. A parallel is the filling in of an income tax return and its interpretation by the Inland Revenue Inspector. The difficulty of the public in filling in a form designed for simplicity, the problems of the Inspector in sorting out genuine from bogus claims and the general puzzling out of how the other party responded or will respond to the questions and answers gives a good idea of the design difficulties and the interaction, even when there has been no personal contact.

There is, however, the extra factor in the interview of the two personalities involved. Interaction now is not only structured by the questions, but by personal feelings. The choice between questionnaires and interviews is usually determined by the high cost of the latter, but it is, once again, also a choice between reliability and insight. Adjustments can be made in interviews and answers can be probed. The cost is in reliability, for if the same interview was done by another interviewer the chance of identical results would usually be low. Agencies like the Government Social Survey obtain high reliability by sticking to set questions and probes, but few organisations are so scrupulous, few studies lend themselves to such rigid questions and there is always the effect of non-verbal clues intervening.

A tale by Blackburn serves to illustrate the need for caution over the validity and permanence of answers from questions.[2] A month after the publication of the influential and carefully designed study of affluent workers at Vauxhalls in Luton, maintaining that 77 per cent of workers were contented with management and working conditions, there was an open revolt with the singing of the Red Flag, a storming of management offices and threats of lynching the directors. The opinions expressed in answer to questions may be short-lived and shallow, but once written into articles and books, or incorporated into lectures they acquire a permanence that belies their actual instability. There are quick profits to be made from questionnaires. Productivity can be boosted by the use of computers. The consumer needs the protection of a few basic guides to quality.

Was there a pilot study?

Whenever questions are to be asked and a choice made from a limited list of answers it is a safeguard if they are tried out in advance. This is a way to avoid many of the mistakes described in the rest of this chapter. The trial run checks that the questions are feasible for the sample. Pilot studies are essential for ensuring that the responses offered as possible answers actually do exhaust all the possibilities. Only by giving a free choice at this stage can all the possible answers be gauged. Some questions may be found useless as the range of answers will be limitless. Others will be found to force similar choices on everyone. Others will be beyond the understanding of the sample. Others will be greeted with derision.

Ideally the answer offered should exhaust all the possibilities and not overlap with each other. In practice respondents often find it difficult to choose an answer that fits their views. Similarly the 'don't know' answer may be found to be used not only by the ignorant, but by those who can not find an answer that fits their attitudes. This type of feasibility study in advance usually combines a check on possible questions with free-ranging unstructured questions allowing the pilot sample to give their own views on the subject under study. In some cases the open-ended enquiry may form a first pilot study and the actual testing of questions a second stage. Without any pilot stage, the actual research is likely to address unsuitable questions to bewildered people.

How long was it?

A skilled interviewer may be able to sustain interest and cooperation through a long session. Sessions of six to eight hours have been achieved.[3] At the other extreme, long postal question-naires are probably never the basis of published work as not even the usual 30 per cent survive the wastepaper basket. The actual length depends on the nature of the sample and the motivation created by the topic. The span of attention of children increases only slowly with age. Old people tire easily. Head teachers, business men and the upper middle class are impatient with any form that may be time-wasting. The span of interest may increase with education but so does scepticism.

How difficult were the questions?

Questions can be too technical or complex. Payne reports trick questions producing support for fictitious Acts and even obtained a substantial percentage in favour of incest.[4] People are wary of admitting ignorance of an issue. The slightest clue will then be used as a guide to an answer. Some words have no precise meaning. The establishment, democracy and big business can raise emotions but obscure issues. 'Fair' is not an alternative answer to 'good' or 'bad', as it has many meanings. The author was once alerted to a survey that indicated an alarming increase in spirit-drinking among schoolchildren. The university department concerned had found many children going to the toilets for a whisky. Fortunately this was corrected before publication as all the teachers concerned knew that this was local slang for masturbation. Once again there is the tendency for social scientists to impose their definitions on terms which have their own everyday meaning.

Even when words are straightforward, they can form a question that can baffle the public. In long questions asking for a choice between alternatives, the last is more often chosen because the first has been forgotten. A good criterion if the actual questions are available in the article or book is to check that they can be understood. The author should not be given the benefit of the doubt unless it was a survey of the sophisticated. Readers of social science are more than usually articulate and often are skilled in sorting out the obscure. The general public who are the usual respondents would flounder where the initiated are merely perplexed.

Could the questions have suggested the answers?

Controversy 6 in this book is a study of attitudes towards religious education. Two surveys carried out by the same research organisation produced completely opposed results, each supporting the conflicting parties that sponsored them. It is not that leading questions are deliberately used, but that it is very difficult not to use them. This is why groups for or against legal abortion, the Common Market, capital punishment, blood sports and the Sunday opening of Welsh pubs can produce convincing evidence to support their case by taking to the streets with a questionnaire. This is rarely dishonest. It is sometimes technical incompetence. It is often innocence of the ease with which questions can be asked to get the results that are wanted.

The following question was the basis of an article maintaining that large numbers of reluctant teachers were entering colleges of education.[5] 'If you were quite free to choose, and could obtain the qualifications necessary, what field of employment would you ideally like to enter?' Fifty-three per cent of the students in colleges of education to whom this question was put indicated some profession other than teaching. Yet given the nature of the question it is remarkable that any opted for teaching. It is not known whether any other professional group would have this or any other degree of commitment for the authors did not provide this basis for comparison.

Was prestige or emotion involved?

Advertisers exploit the ease with which people can be led to associate themselves with the prestigeful. All the best people soak their teeth overnight in X after seducing their girl friend with gin and Y tonic. It may not seem decent to admit that the wogs begin at Boulogne and it is better to say you read the *Spectator* than *Playboy*. Questions can easily lead people to choose right not real answers. Furthermore, there may always be a reluctance to use the 'don't know' category. None of us likes to be made to seem ignorant, especially about an issue that the man with the schedule obviously thinks important.

Could the environment have influenced the answers?

Where questions are asked about life in schools, old people's homes, prisons or other relatively closed organisations, there may be pressure to give answers within a particular context. Again right not real answers appear. The author, comparing responses from the same students on questionnaires and interviews in a college of education, had to scrap the use of unverified questionnaires because students were giving the answers they thought students in training should give.[6] Only when group discussions were held to examine the discrepancy in answers was this innocent deception uncovered. Yet combinations of methods facilitating such cross-checking are rare. Usually a single instrument is considered enough.

When were answers pre-coded?

Questions can be unstructured, giving the respondent a free rein to answer at will, or structured, giving him only a choice of answers listed by the researcher. In the first case the researcher takes the answers and sorts them out into categories after collection. In the latter type this categorisation is done before the start of data collection. In both cases the researcher is imposing his social scientific framework around the possible common sense answers of his respondents. There is rarely a perfect fit. There is usually a pruning and bending to make the irregular everyday responses fit into the categories prepared for them. This happens in both sequences. But leaving the categorisation to the end by using open-ended, unstructured questions leaves a lot to the discretion of the researcher or his coding staff, and this particular Procrustean bed is hidden from the reader.

The dangers of using questionnaires can best be illustrated by looking at the best research designs. The Authoritarian Personality studies have been subject to detailed analysis by Hyman and Sheatsley.[7] They acknowledge that it has hardly been rivalled for scope, prestige and influence. The work combined questionnaires and clinical interviews, the former being used to select extreme scorers on scales measuring potential Fascism for detailed analysis.

The questionnaires were first tried out on students and then adults in 1945. Hyman and Sheatsley maintain that despite the careful design the questions forced subjects to choose extreme answers without having the scope to qualify these. Yet this lack of qualification was later taken as an indication of a tendency to stereotype minority groups. By limiting the choice, the researchers produced extreme responses and then pointed out the significance of this polarisation.

The Institute of Race Relation's scale for measuring tolerance reported in Controversy 11 was criticised in a similar way for having a built-in bias towards tolerance. The difficulty here is that one man's tolerance is another's prejudice. Even more significant, Frenkel-Brunswick, one of the authors of the Authoritarian Personality, looking back at the research after a decade had passed, recognised that she and her colleagues were probably influenced by the anti-Fascist climate of opinion in the immediate post-1945 years.[8] Questions about sensitive areas of human experience are difficult to word neutrally. Even if this is accomplished the results are probably invalid within a short period as the words summing up these results will have changed.

Interviews

Interviews not only depend on the quality of the questions asked, but on the awareness of, and control over, the interaction involved. The interview can be more flexible than the questionnaire, it can probe deeper, can be adjusted to circumstances, can increase rapport and cooperation. But the cost may be a reduction in control and consequently in reliability. As these issues are discussed in the following pages, it must be remembered that there is always interaction involved in the filling in of questionnaires.

The way clues can be incidentally presented and skilfully interpreted can be gauged from Pfungst's investigation of Clever Hans, a horse that could apparently solve mathematical problems, spell and identify musical notes by nodding his head, tapping his feet or pointing to letters on a board.[9] Public and experts were baffled and his master, Van Osten, a schoolmaster, made no profit from the act. Pfungst, by diligently controlling factors in the environment of the performance, found that although Clever Hans could answer even when the question was not even spoken, the questioner had to be present and seen by the horse. He noticed how tense the questioner got as the horse appeared to start to tap or point to the right answer. Pfungst now saw what all animal trainers rely on, that the horse could detect these slight involuntary clues. Pfungst even learned the trick himself so that, on all fours and blindfolded, he could answer questions from his audience without them being spoken. If a horse can detect such muscular movements as clues, man, the symbol-using animal must respond to much more than mere questions in an interview situation.

If the reader can get past the substance of the Kinsey Reports to the sections on method, they will find an acid test of interviewing.[10] It was necessary to stop any tendency to brag or distort as the sample were volunteers. Many indeed seemed to want to measure their sexual prowess against others. Complete confidentiality, absolute privacy during interviewing and no suggestions of right and wrong behaviour were the guides to rapport. Kinsey himself carried out 7,000 interviews lasting an hour to an hour and a half. This labour of love was conducted deadpan; friendly, but never with any expression of surprise or disapproval.

The questions were asked as directly as possible to avoid interaction. The interviewer looked squarely at the subject and moved inexorably from factual background to intimate detail. Questions were fired rapidly, giving little time to think. Frank sexual terms were used. When abnormal behaviour was being probed it was 'How many times?', not 'Do you . . . ?' Questions were used to check others, husbands were checked against wives, reinterviewing after eighteen months was employed. This study is acknowledged as classic. Its weaknesses are in its sampling rather than the method of interviewing. It is important, however, to remember that the questions were about actual sexual behaviour not attitudes towards it. The reports give little salacious pleasure and are a reliable guide for the same reasons.

Were the interviewers trained?

Kinsey and his three associates memorised the coding system of their interview schedules so that subjects saw only symbols being recorded. Most reputable research agencies have some form of selection and training programmes for their interviewers. The Government Social Survey uses only standardised, structured interviews. Because design is by experts and questions are piloted, the interviewers have to follow the wording of the schedules. Some latitude is allowed over factual questions, but with attitude questions there can be repetition but no alteration. Even prompts are written into the schedules and stock phrases are provided for probing obscure answers.[11]

Obviously with such care over design and such control over the interviewers, training is necessary. Moser reports that only 16 per cent of applicants finally passed all tests and went on to actual training in 1953.[12] Applicants are sent a handbook to study in advance and invited to attend a three-day initial training class. Those accepted after this go into the field with a training officer who demonstrates the method and observes early attempts. If successful a probationary period is entered during which supervision is provided. Then a written test is given on the principles in the handbook. Trial interviews are recorded to check reliability. Even when fully trained and experienced there is still supervision by training officers. Once on the job these interviewers know how to approach subjects, how and where to sit, the tone of the voice to use and the time to bring out the schedules.

Government Social Survey workers have to be particular because of the importance of the subject matter they handle. But this care illustrates the gap between the best and the worst. Many market research organisations have no selection procedures and little training. It is common to use students from social science departments both as training for them and as ways of gathering data for research. Anyone who has interviewed, canvassed or even tried to get factual information from strangers knows that the apparent incomprehension of many people is boundless. In addition the interaction can range from hostility, through indifference to seduction. Training at least alerts the innocent.

The success of training has been illustrated by Durbin and Stuart.[13] Here experienced Government Social Survey and experienced British Institute of Public Opinion interviewers were compared with another sample of inexperienced students. There was a striking and consistent difference in the proportion of schedules that were successfully completed. The experienced got more filled in, received fewer refusals, and reported fewer 'gone away'.

How much control?

The Government Social Survey exercises rigid control over its interviewers. Kinsey and colleagues adjusted questions to suit the subjects. A solitary interviewer like Zweig sees his work as always a pilot study, always open to the importance of the chance remark to follow up.[14] Questions are varied between subjects and the aim is to produce an informal relaxed relationship. To Zweig interviewing must be a two-way traffic. His own description of his technique highlights spontaneity, curiosity and joyfulness.

It is often difficult to find any description of the conditions of interviewing in published accounts. Where none is given it may be safer to assume that little trouble was taken to control the conditions for the interviews. Yet there are techniques available apart from careful training. Coding can be reduced to simple signs to avoid long pauses. Tape and video recorders can be used, enabling the interview to be checked later on by a second judge. Most subjects rapidly forget a tape recorder is present and cassette machines are inconspicuous.

Finally it is best to be cautious about results from interviews produced by a single researcher. Here the obvious danger is that by tone of voice, anticipatory gestures or some other action that Clever Hans as well as humans skilled in giving and interpreting cues could recognise, the eager researcher will get the answers he wants. Checks by second parties, the use of neutral interviewers can help. At least there should be some cautionary remarks to warn the lay reader of the dangers of self-fulfilling interviews.

Who was being interviewed?

It has already been suggested that interviewing within organisations might be affected by particular circumstances, making generalisations hazardous. But other groups are likely to respond to interviewers in ways that introduce bias. Rich has pointed to the authority of an adult when interviewing children.[15] The child will be likely to seize on an answer rather than telling the whole truth. To Holt, a child's response to teaching is usually a game to deceive by acting docile, looking attentive, acting silly and so on.[16] If skilled teachers are fooled, interviewers will have little chance of learning the game. This is especially the case with difficult questions where children are reluctant to answer 'don't know' and will grab at any hints offered. Part of the skill of being a pupil is to be able to detect clues and give the answer the adult wants even though it was not understood. Another difficulty is in communication. To phrase questions in words understandable by children is difficult, and there is a tendency to try to overcome this by speaking to them as if they were rather dense foreigners, thus further increasing the artificiality of the situation and the motive of the child to play the game this apparently simple-minded interviewer wants.

Old people are similarly prone to grab at answers and to answer irrelevantly.[17] They are also liable to grab the interviewer and involve him in some personal gossip. The interviewer is often someone to talk to, or from whom to get advice or sympathy. The interviewer struggles to get his question in against the old person's attempt to introduce his own problems. The old, like the young, are not likely to tell the interviewer to push off but are likely to suck him into their own personal world. In these cases the danger in the impact of everyday and scientific constructions of reality is that the former will engulf the latter, leaving the interviewer with the job of making some sense of the data in his terms once he has escaped from his subject.

The interaction that links questions and answers

The questionnaire and the interview involve interaction between researcher and respondent. The interaction ranges from the impersonal postal questionnaire, to the intimate, unstructured interview. But in every case there is a meeting of different definitions of the same situation, whether the respondents are willing or reluctant. Given the majority who dispose of postal questionnaires into the waste bin, it can be assumed that many who agree to be interviewed do so with reluctance. The answers received will be affected by this interaction as well as by the questions asked.

The choice of methods of asking questions is not only determined by the researcher's concern to get beneath surface responses to the meanings given to situations. Clearly there would be no point in using unstructured interviews for the Census, nor in trying to use postal questionnaires in a study of fiddling at work. The researcher makes a choice after considering the cost, the resources available, the time in which the data has to be collected, as well as the subject matter and the likely balance of reliability and validity. There may be occasions when a questionnaire, because it reduces interaction, may obtain more valid results than an interview. Kinsey's brisk interviewing style probably obtained more valid results than would some more intimate tête à tête over sexual behaviour.[18] There is a general guide that the unstructured interview is probably the most informative, but in the hands of the unskilled is liable to be the most disastrous.[19] The structured interview is safer for the amateur. Similarly, an unwary or unscrupulous researcher can extract any information desired from an unstructured questionnaire, but less damage is likely through biased interpretation when the questions are tightly structured. Facilitating interaction increases the chance of validity, but makes it more difficult to obtain reliability.

The interview and the questionnaire are the most important means of collecting information in the social sciences. The methodological problems in their use also lie at the centre of the differences between those who focus primarily on behaviour and those who look first at the meanings given to events by those involved. The use of structured questionnaires and interviews is opposed by the latter because they are the means of imposing meanings on respondents. They inhibit the use of just the taken-for-granted, everyday terms that those concerned with understanding how people make sense of the world are looking for. Similarly the training of interviewers is a way of ensuring that the imposed structure remains intact. Even probes to produce answers when the respondent doesn't reply are seen as further instruments for imposing the researcher's interpretation of the situation on those being studied. Because there is interaction in the interview or when filling in a questionnaire, the positivist imposes preconceived categories and terms. Because that imposition inhibits the production of everyday interpretations, concepts and language, the social phenomenologist or symbolic interactionist sees it resulting in a deceptive, bogus objectivity.

In practice, researchers who know their trade are aware of the dangers of distortion through structuring and of unreliability through lack of structure. Thus J. and E. Newson, investigating the sensitive area of child-rearing, used the interview to get information from the mother, in her home.[20] They developed a technique that created an unrestrained climate in which the mother would talk freely about her child. What the mother said was seen as important. The tape-recorder was used as a way in which this climate could be retained; it enabled the interviewer to give all her attention to the mother. Because there was no need to write down the significant contributions from the mothers they were less inhibited. But information was pencilled into the interview schedules to limit the time needed to transcribe the tapes later on. They describe this sensitive interviewing as an art form. There must be a genuine interest in the responses given so that the interviewer as expert still retains a natural, unforced interview situation. Here the interview was being used to gather information in an area important for public policy. The problems revolving around control and spontaneity at the theoretical level were thought through in the Newsons' work as a result of the practical situation faced. There is nothing surprising in this coincidence of theoretical and practical concern. Asking questions and getting answers involves interaction. The nature of that interaction is at the heart of sociology and social psychology. But it is also a central concern of researchers involved in producing evidence to affect policy. In both cases a balance is being sought between reliability through control and validity through spontaneity.

TO STREAM OR UNSTREAM?

This controversy illustrates the difficulty of obtaining conclusive answers to practical problems through research, even where the design problems appear to be small. But it also shows how evidence can be interpreted to present a case which is more formidable than warranted.

In the 1930s streaming was introduced into most elementary schools. This grouping by ability was soon supported by evidence from educational psychology. The attack on streaming opened in the 1950s. This was part of a general attack on selection procedures, secondary organisation as well as streaming. It has been notable for the vigour and organisation of the parties involved. It soon stimulated a movement in defence of the established system, making it difficult for the lay reader, not knowing the allegiance of the writer, to judge the reliability of the evidence used. Only in 1970 was a large-scale, adequately controlled and neutral investigation published.[1] It was predictably inconclusive.

The first campaign for de-streaming opened in the magazine *Forum*. De-streaming soon became a popular research topic. The first evidence came from Finch (1954),[2] Rudd (1956),[3] Blandford (1958),[4] Morris (1959),[5] and Daniels (1959).[6] Finch, Blandford and Daniels favoured de-streaming. Morris found streaming beneficial for the teaching of reading and Rudd detected little difference in the two methods. In 1959 Yates and Pidgeon from the neutral position of the National Foundation cautioned readers about drawing conclusions from these early and poorly controlled studies.[7]

The zenith of the reformers came in 1964. *Forum* held a

conference, submitted evidence to the Plowden committee and published a paperback, *Non-Streaming in the Junior School.*[8] In this year Douglas published *The Home and the School* reporting that streaming reinforced social selection within the schools.[9] Finally Jackson condemned streaming as discriminatory and unjust.[10] The shortcomings of the Douglas study have already been discussed. Jackson drew extensively on Daniels and used personal interpretation rather than detached investigation as a method.

Only after 1964 was the attitude of the teachers controlled in the experiments. In the Plowden Report streaming was shown to lead to higher attainment. De-streaming was favoured, but only if the attitudes of teachers and the organisation of learning were favourable. Finally in 1970 a major study for the National Foundation for Educational Research was published.[11] Here 5,500 children in seventy-two junior schools were studied. With the controls built into this research no clear conclusions were drawn. Given enthusiastic, skilful teachers, non-streaming had advantages, particularly for the motivation of children. But even in unstreamed schools about half the teachers still supported streaming. Increased control over this influence had here led to decreased certainty.

This tendency for reliability and certainty to be inversely proportional appears in all the major studies. In the USA, not only is the most carefully controlled experiment inconclusive,[12] but a review of all available American research could also detect nothing definite.[13] In Sweden a summary of the available investigations suggested that streaming produced slightly better results in academic achievement.[14] Finally a review of evidence from many countries concluded that streaming could not be explained in solely educational terms, but was essentially a reflection of the organisation of society.[15] This review of international evidence also concluded that conclusive evidence was unlikely ever to be collected as the variables involved were too complicated for adequate control. The attitude of the teachers was the most important and the most difficult to control. It was also the link between the organisation of the society and the organisation of learning.

•The failure to produce conclusive evidence over a method of organising schoolchildren where controlled experiment is possible and the subjects unlikely to distort the results deliberately indicates the limits of social scientific research as a reliable source for decision-making. Few areas of research present such an apparently simple design problem. Yet the efforts of researchers in many countries to improve design to answer the question of streaming or non-streaming have only led to greater certainty that the results will be inconclusive.

This is not the impression given to students or the lay public. The research has been used as a weapon, not a flashlight. It took twenty years in England for a major study to be published after the start of a campaign backed by small-scale research. Excluding the cautious evidence of Douglas, the accounts appearing in books are heavily selective. Of all the small-scale studies, the most quoted is that of Daniels, which was also the most favourable towards de-streaming. Indeed, no other research has produced such strong evidence for the academic as well as the social benefits of de-streaming. This is the one higher degree thesis which is extensively quoted by students in examination answers. Yet this was only a pioneering study by an enthusiastic egalitarian of two pairs of junior schools with negligible controls. The conclusions about the brighter and duller children were inevitably based on very few children. It is significant that Daniels's study was chosen for replication by the Surrey Educational Research Association.[16] The report, published in 1968, came to the opposite conclusions. Here achievement in streamed schools was significantly higher. The same methods produced opposite results.

It is easy to be too dismissive of this research to establish whether streaming is beneficial or harmful. The inconclusiveness of the comparisons between streamed and unstreamed classes is itself important. It confirms that no single organisational change is going to make all that difference. It dampens down the protagonists. Particularly in the case of the Barker Lunn study it brings out the importance of the attitudes of teachers. If they are luke-warm, de-streaming is unlikely to work. The confirmation of the importance of this evidence, however disappointing it is not to show conclusively that de-streaming is a disaster or a success, lies in the response to Barker Lunn's research.[17] The evidence may have been neutral, but 'streamers' and 'non-streamers' attacked it with equal vigour. The function of social research is often to show that human organisation is rarely either good or bad, efficient or disastrous, but dependent on many complicated human factors. It is important to check the over-simplification of complex human issues.

7

EXPERIMENTS

Much social science is legitimately concerned with describing behaviour, or with understanding the ways in which humans comprehend their world. But even when a researcher explicitly denies that it is possible to establish causes and find laws of human behaviour, there is still a concern about how and why social situations develop. Thus Hargreaves, Hester and Mellor, examining *Deviance in Classrooms*, state that they were working within a 'phenomenological' rather than a 'positivist' paradigm.[1] Their concern was to show how rules develop as a taken-for-granted feature of classrooms, the way teachers define certain pupils as troublemakers, and the reaction of those teachers to disruptive conduct. How do teachers define some acts as deviant? How do teachers define some pupils as deviant? The answers are given from the viewpoint of pupils and teachers. Yet the authors, while avoiding talk of causes, try to explain how teachers cope with disruption. They develop two principles showing how teachers anticipate and treat disruption, and then justify their actions. They explain how and why teachers act in typical ways. It may be worth preserving a distinction between explanatory principles and causes, but few readers will appreciate the subtlety. In practice the main differences between positivist and phenomenological research are in the approach and design, not in the conclusions. As soon as the accounts of those involved are interpreted by the researcher, and the reasons for the phenomena studied are explained, all are concerned with 'how' and 'why'.

The natural science way to causes and to prediction is through experimentation. The diagram that follows shows the simplest controlled experimental design.

	Observation	Intervention	Observation
Experimental sample	1a ———→	(cause) ———→	2a
Control sample	1b ————————————————————→		2b

1a and 1b could be observations of identical empty gas jars. The intervention could be to fill one of these with damp beans. 2a and 2b are observations made after a few days have passed. Any differences observed at the end of the experiment can be attributed to the insertion of the beans. The confidence in this conclusion depends on the control exerted to ensure that all conditions were identical for experimental and control gas jar, apart from the insertion of the beans. Extraneous factors have been controlled. There are many variations on this basic design, but it is the model from which causes can be inferred and predictions made.

The difficulties in even approaching the control exercised in this model have been illustrated in this chapter. Even in experimental laboratory research, human interaction can defeat attempts to control, although a social psychologist such as Sherif has imaginatively extended our understanding of perception and the production of norms by experimental design in a natural situation.[2] Away from the laboratory the degree of control will diminish further. In addition to the rejection of this model by large numbers of social scientists, there are great difficulties in implementing anything approximating to it. Nevertheless it is a useful model. Comparisons with the control sample 1b and 2b enables the researcher to be confident that extraneous factors did not cause the phenomena observed. Secondly, the causal, explanatory or independent variable is clearly defined. This makes this design ideal for testing 'if X, then Y' type hypotheses.

The social scientist rarely uses such designs outside the laboratory. But variations on it are common. For example, one of the high points of positivistic research into delinquency was S. and E. Glueck's *Unraveling Juvenile Delinquency*.[3] This employed an experimental group of 500 and another control group of the same number. The former were delinquents who were matched on a number of social factors with the non-delinquent control group. Obviously these factors used to match the groups were consequently not available as possible causes. Comparisons were then made of factors, such as parental control, expected to be important, to see if the two groups differed. On the basis of these comparisons, prediction scales were produced, and used, to identify children who were at risk of becoming delinquent. Such research, once very popular, is now rare. The major problem is that the non-delinquent control children were probably as naughty as the experimental group, but either had not been caught, or had committed crimes which had not interested the police. Nevertheless this experimental work has given us a number of generally accepted hypotheses about the factors behind delinquency which are now part of the folklore.

In education the approximation to the classical design had been very close where innovations have been evaluated. There is a copious literature over the merits and snags in adopting this model as distinct from formative illuminative designs that are not experimental, but rely on observing processes rather than products. The evaluation of streaming is in the experimental tradition.[4] The studies of football supporters are ethnographic, retaining the natural situation and depending on observation.[5] The most suspect design in educational research is the before and after study without any control groups. If a new way of teaching reading is introduced, it may seem sufficient to test a few classes before and after to see if the new way has been effective. But if a difference is found, it is impossible to be confident that it has resulted from the innovation. Teachers using new methods may put more into their work, extraneous factors may account for the difference, the children may have matured across the time of the innovation, the second test after the innovation may have been affected by practice on the first some time earlier, absences among good or bad readers could have made a difference, the tests may be unreliable and second, follow-up test results are affected by regression to the mean.

Even where control groups are used some of these factors may still be affecting results. Many are difficult to control when humans are the subject of the research. For example, a common cause of distortion of results is difference between experimental and control groups at the start. Ideally these should be identical before the experiment so that differences afterwards can be attributed to the causal, independent variable. But there are usually objections to allocating pupils to both experimental and to control groups.

Teachers can simultaneously object to exposing their children to an innovation, while maintaining that it is unfair that the control group should be denied the new experience. The ideal way of forming groups where large numbers are involved is by random allocation. But school classes are usually formed before the researcher can persuade teachers to form them at random. Another method is to form groups in which the children are matched for background factors such as intelligence, sex and social background. But usually the researcher falls back on existing school classes as his experimental and control groups. This increases the chance that there will not be a genuine comparison of identical groups and that extraneous factors may account for any observed differences after the intervention. The reader should look carefully at this formation of groups. Where existing groups have been used there should have been some check on the similarity of the groups on some of the more important background factors that could affect the results.

These difficulties in quasi-experimental research account for the disappointing results obtained in evaluating educational innovations such as the Educational Priority Area schemes in Britain, or Head Start Programmes in the United States.[6] The results are often not statistically significant. The researchers have however done their best to evaluate small investments into large problems, so striking results should be unexpected. Even more difficult for the researcher has been the difficulty in establishing what the intervention was supposed to be. A look at the Plowden Report which recommended E.P.A.s gives no detail on the precise measures that were to be taken or the objectives to be attained. The experiment can be a powerful tool in evaluation and in getting at causes. Above all, it can give the reader, and researchers that follow, a clear idea of the extent to which extraneous factors have been controlled. It is likely to be more reliable than other designs, but its greatest asset is that there are well-tried experimental designs. They may not produce valid evidence, and the extent of control, while increasing reliability, may make the situation so artificial that generalisation is impossible. But an experimental design gives the reader, and, later researchers, the best chance of receiving an understandable account of the research design. The design may be flawed, but there is a chance to assess it.

Experimental effect

The effect of being involved in an experiment was first observed in the studies of the Hawthorne works of the General Electric Company in Chicago between 1924 and 1927.[7] These studies, initially concerned with productivity, were organised by Mayo at the Harvard Graduate School of Business and have been responsible for a shift in emphasis within industrial psychology. They have also provided the foundations for the human relations school of management. The reason for the lasting influence of these studies despite criticisms of their design will be discussed later.[8] Their importance here is the detection of the impact of being involved in an experiment on the workers in the factory. After experimental manipulation of the material conditions of work it was concluded that productivity depended primarily on the human relations involved and that the interest shown in the workers by the experimenters was the main factor behind their extra efforts. · Indeed, even the deliberate worsening of material conditions of work seemed to have resulted in extra production due to the worker's feeling of being of concern to someone in authority. While these assumptions have been challenged on political as well as methodological grounds, the actual impact on the subjects of experimentation has been repeatedly confirmed.

This is often referred to as Hawthorne, or experimental effect. People under observation do not behave normally, but respond to the experimental conditions. The Hawthorne workers responded in a way that defeated the original purpose of the experiment and initiated a series of further investigations into the human relations that were influencing productivity and turnover of labour. An extraneous variable, initially unrecognised and therefore uncontrolled, had intervened and in many cases proved more influential than the variable of physical environment originally being manipulated. Experiments on humans are always subject to this effect which, if not controlled, may bias results.

One example of this can be seen in a recent experiment designed to involve parents in the affairs of a school to see if this improved the attainment of the children.[9] Children were tested for attainment before and after the experimental programme and in two other schools used as controls. However, the effect of the programme could not be compared with the control schools because these had reacted to the tests by drawing up new schemes of work, employing extra teachers and concentrating on improving the performance of the children on the tests. This unintended consequence of selecting schools for testing was named by the authors the Bethnal Green effect, after the Hawthorne effect that was the first indication of distortion caused by involvement in an experiment rather than by any impact of the selected variables. In the Bethnal Green case the effect was probably heightened by the status of the research directors. When notables and even university departments ask schools to join a project or experiment, Hawthorne effect is inevitable.

This effect has been demonstrated experimentally. As early as 1936 Canady, himself a black, showed how white and black children scored differently on intelligence tests when tested by white and black testers.[10] A white child tested first by a black and then by a white tester two or three weeks later gained I.Q. points. Black children tested first by black and then by a white tester dropped I.Q. points, despite the practice gained. Only in the 1960s was this type of study taken up again and there have been many confirmations that the colour of the tester makes a difference. Doubtless the current relations between the races is also an important factor.

Obviously if intelligence test scores are influenced by the interaction of tester and tested, personality tests will be even more vulnerable. One obvious influence would be sex and sex appeal. Rabin, Nelson and Clark arranged for males to wait in a room decorated with anatomical charts.[11] There was no difference when they were then tested by males or females. But a sample of men left waiting in a room decorated with pictures of nude women gave significantly more sexual responses to Rorschach ink blot when tested by men compared with women. While somewhat removed from general practice, this does indicate the importance of the sex of the tester. Furthermore, interpreting ink blots is hardly likely to arouse erotic feelings and other tasks might have produced even greater differences.

More reliable, if less enjoyable to take part in, was an experiment by Masling using eight postgraduate students to try out sentence completion projective techniques on two attractive female

undergraduates.[12] These two women played warm and cold roles
as they were tested. They had previously memorised two sets of
responses to the sentence completion tests with equal numbers of
sick and healthy responses. Their interactions with the testers were
taped to check that their responses were the same with each tester.
Each tester saw one of the girls in a cold and one in a warm role.
They then wrote up their reports. Masling found that the testers
made more positive statements about the girl who had acted
warmly towards him and shown an interest in him than about the
girl who acted cold.

This experimental check on the influence of a tester's response
to the friendliness and sexual promise of the subject was also used
by Masling to check scoring on the Wechsler-Bellevue intelligence
tests.[13] Here the warm subjects were scored more leniently, were
given more opportunity to clarify or correct responses and were
given more encouragement during the test.

There is one other effect of being involved in an experiment that
is important in assessing evidence from laboratory work. Orne has
suggested that the fact of being involved in a psychological
experiment is itself a source of influence on response.[14] Thus in
experiments on hypnosis, Orne maintains that the setting itself
gave the subjects a feeling of being part of an impressive, solemn
experience that created effects that were impossible to separate from
the hypnotic stimulus being used. They did their best to make the
experiment succeed. Friedman has also pointed out that this
confusion of experimenter and stimulus has always occurred in
studies of hypnosis.[15] Mesmer himself must have credited his
apparatus with powers of hypnosis that were actually his own.
Mesmerism was confused with mechanically produced hypnosis.
What experimenters do incidentally may be confused with the
experimental stimulus they manipulate. It is necessary, therefore,
to investigate, not only the effect of being involved in experimentation, but the effects introduced accidentally by the experimenter.
This is another hole in the controls.

Experimenter effect

In the ideal experiment there are simply subject and stimulus under the control of, but not influenced by, an experimenter. But in experiments with humans, interaction is inevitable. The researcher cannot remain neutral however hard he tries to standardise his actions. He greets the subjects, settles them down, varies his words, gestures and expressions, just as they vary theirs. The experimenter steps out of his role to become interested in a pretty girl, to put a shy person at ease, to stop a child crying or comfort an old lady. In doing so he is breaching his controls over himself and making himself a factor in the experiment. He is giving clues to his subjects through which they can interpret the situation and get an idea how to respond.

Rosenthal, in his book *Experimenter Effects in Behavioural Research*,[16] provides plentiful evidence of such extraneous variables, including his own experiments devised to test the effect on results of the expectations of the experimenter. In this work there is no indication of how these expectations were communicated to the subjects, but the process may be similar to that described previously where the owners of clever animals or mind readers managed to convey the requisite answer. If this is the case it is particularly relevant for experiments in education, for children in school are prepared to look for clues about correct answers.

Friedman, working with Rosenthal, gives a clue to the way influence is exerted. He filmed twenty-nine experimenters at work with eighty-six subjects on a perception test to see if uncontrolled influences were at work.[17] Observers then saw the films and filled in scales on the number of glances and smiles passing between experimenters and subject, another relating to the dress of the experimenter and noted whether he was wearing glasses or not. The behaviour of each experimenter was then related to the results of the experiment. The first result was that the experimenters behaved very differently. The second was that the way the experimenter behaved was an influence on how the subject answered. The exchange of glances and the time taken over the parts of the experiment were particularly influential.

Thus experiments differ in the degree to which they are controlled and a written account of the arrangements may leave out many uncontrolled influences arising out of the behaviour of the experimenter and his interaction with the subjects of the experiment. In a world in which the experimenter has an aura of professionalism that tends to impress, subjects are liable to over-cooperate. Orne has pointed particularly at the college student who appears as the subject of many experiments and who may be motivated to support a hypothesis, skilled at guessing what it is from the nature of the experiment and alert to the clues that the experimenter may provide about the answers that are needed for success.[18] Like many people in doctor's surgeries, subjects in a laboratory are keen to be good cooperative patients.

The key to successful and reliable experiment is therefore a sufficient level of control. There are three areas that need controlling, the subjects, the stimuli, and, from what has just been discussed, the experimenter and the environment of which he forms a part. Likely personality and background differences of the subjects can be controlled by control groups matched as near as possible in all but the particular characteristic being investigated or through the random selection of groups. The stimulus can be controlled by standardising his actions as rigidly as possible. But from what has already been said, complete control is impossible in the behavioural sciences, because humans are so adept at obtaining meanings from apparently slight clues.

In the social sciences the most usual experiment takes the present situation as the effect of some past event and then traces back to establish a relation between the two. But the degree of control over the many variables involved tends to be small. It would be interesting to trace the education of successful people to see if factors such as attending public or progressive schools were important. But education is not definable as a single factor and many other influences will have been at work. It may be possible to match groups to eliminate the effect of some of these extraneous factors, but reliability is likely to be low and alternative explanations for the present situation being investigated cannot be eliminated. History, politics, economics and sociology abound with the resulting controversies between rival schools of thought, all claiming support from analysis after the event.

The major obstacle in any *ex post facto* explanation is that the causes indicated could never have been used to predict the event. Everyone theorises about the causes of crime or war by examining past events, but none of the combinations of actors suggested as the cause exhausts all the possible combinations. These explanations are plausible only because the event has already occurred. Such experiments are always inadequate. Different people will choose different factors and give each factor a different weight in the explanation.

THE REFORMATION AND THE SCHOOLS

The controversy that follows is taken from history. It illustrates not only how different selections of evidence can be used to support different causes, but how the same evidence can be used to reinforce or undermine a cause by reporting it within a different context.

Towards the end of the nineteenth century A.F. Leach, working for the Charity Commissioners as they tried to sort out the affairs of the endowed schools, produced a number of articles and books that changed existing ideas on the history of English schools.[1] Leach worked from the surviving records of the chantry commissioners and challenged the accepted view that the grammar schools originated at the Reformation. Indeed he favoured the idea that the Reformation was a disaster for education, destroying the grammar and eliminating the elementary schools. By going back to the original sources he appeared to have corrected a mistaken view of the history of schooling. Partly as a result of this work, Leach was chosen to write or edit the chapters on schools in the *Victoria County Histories*.

While there had been adverse criticism of Leach, the first attack using other documentary evidence came with two articles by Mrs J. Simon in 1955. These criticisms were repeated in her book *Education and Society in Tudor England* published in 1966.[2] Simon's criticisms of Leach were that he lacked historical perspective and artificially abstracted the history of the schools from the general history of the period. In particular he suppressed or ignored evidence that countered his opinions. Consequently Leach overestimated school provision before the Reformation. Simon also suggests that Leach held these views as part of his involvement with the Charity Commissioners in adapting the surviving endowments to form a new system of secondary schools in the late Victorian period.

A vigorous defence of Leach was published in 1963.[3] In this, Chaplin maintained that Simon's criticisms, like many others, were derived from original criticisms forty years before. Furthermore, in his defence of Leach against Simon, there was also an attack on work by Jordan[4] which had seemed to further weaken Leach's argument. Jordan's massive analysis of English philanthropy in the fifteenth and sixteenth centuries built up a strong case for this period as the real starting point of English secondary education on a large scale. But Chaplin argued that Jordan had been influenced by Simon in his views and had misjudged the real evidence presented by Leach. Indeed, despite the criticisms of Leach by Jordan, he still relied on the evidence collected by Leach although, according to Chaplin, not always acknowledging his debt.

The final twist in this controversy can be found in criticisms of the work of Jordan himself. Curiously these mainly concentrate on the very criticisms that Simon had originally levelled against Leach, for Jordan, in making his detailed tabulations of bequests across nearly two centuries, ignored accompanying economic changes. Among these changes the most crucial was a fall in the value of money. Fisher has calculated that had this been taken into account, an apparent dramatic increase in philanthropic aid to schools in the period after the Reformation may have actually been a fall.[5]

These controversies over the use of documents and their interpretation illustrate the difficulties of reaching agreement when the historian can select among the material available and when fresh documentary evidence is liable to be found. The importance of these controversies is not that they show how the political attitudes of the writers affect their use of documents, but that one view often comes to be accepted without sufficient evidence. Once accepted it becomes dogma, unquestioned unless fresh documentary evidence becomes available or there is such a change in the political climate that research guided by new views on old problems is stimulated.

8

DOCUMENTS AND OTHER UNOBTRUSIVE MEASURES

Most books are not based on information gathered for the purpose but are collections of material, often first published in articles, that have been organised by the author to present a new perspective on an issue. Thus articles usually rest on primary sources of data, books on secondary sources and later books on tertiary material from earlier ones. At each step, distance from the original study lends a misleading enchantment to the reliability of the primary source. The original article may have a cautious section on methods, the first book briefly mentions them and later ones just quote the evidence, not how it was obtained. Thus tentative suggestions may become hard facts.

This tendency for doubts about reliability to diminish with the distance from the original also applies to the extraction of evidence from documents. All documents are distant from the reality they may reflect. The Census deals with the basic statistics of the population at a given date. But the data is given by a citizen, tabulated by another and interpreted by the reader. Mistakes can happen. Juvenile parsons frequent some areas and pensioners some schools. When the document is an account which contains interpretations, the distance from reality can be further barricaded by slanted perceptions. *Mein Kampf* would not be studied as a dependable historical document, but it was only one stage removed from the conditions that Hitler was observing. Other documents are secondary in being written by an author after interpreting other documents. There can be a long chain of such interpretations. At each stage the chance of bias increases.

The distance between document and reality, and the number of interpretations involved have to be considered in interpreting

documentary evidence. Even research reports have to be interpreted with caution. A local education authority may want
information on the state of its schools. It instructs its inspectors
and advisers to collect the data. The collected information is sorted
through by a senior inspector and a selection of reports
summarised. The report then goes in draft to colleagues. Informal
consultations take place with political members. Suggestions are
received and revisions made. A draft goes to education committee
and after amendments, a version is made public. Even before the
document becomes available it may have become an instrument for
change, a support for policies, a reflection of professional opinion
rather than an image of reality. All documents go through similar
stages. This is no different from the sequence of interpretations
that link the start of an idea for research, through the collection of
data, to the preparation and publication of a report.

In sociology, the user of documents has also to take notice of the
phenomenological view outlined in Chapter 9. The police, the
courts, doctors, teachers and so on produce reports which at every
stage of processing identify and confirm people as delinquents, or
sick or under-attaining. Individuals are slotted into categories. The
coding of data for processing by computer is a typical categorising
procedure, often involving mutilation to obtain a fit. Documents
are problematic. To Cicourel each report must be treated as a
particular interpretation within a particular situation. His book,
The Social Organization of Juvenile Justice,[1] uses records, but not as
a source of information on delinquents, but to show how they come
to be defined as delinquent. With this view, even the report full of
statistical tables must be seen as a particular way of categorising,
not as some immutable, consistent and agreed formulation. The
assessment of evidence derived from documents requires the same
basic questions to be answered as with all forms of research. The
test of reliability is still whether another researcher would extract
the same information from the available documents. There is still a
need to assess whether enough care has been taken to ensure that
superfluous information has not been taken as central. Finally the
extent to which the information that has been extracted can be
generalised has to be determined. Reliability and validity are still
central issues.

Gottschalk, reviewing the use of personal documents in history, selects as the first problem for the historian the establishment of the authenticity of the document.[2] Second, if the document is reliable, the credibility of the evidence in it has to be determined. The historian adopts the attitude of the lawyer towards evidence, questioning the ultimate source of the evidence, the ability and honesty of the witness and the accuracy with which he has been reported in the document. Finally he looks for corroboration by independent sources. Third, the historian has to assess the relevance of the information. It is useful historically only if it relates to other history rather than standing as an isolated incident, however interesting.

Thus Gottschalk is asking whether the text is genuine, and if so, what is it really saying. However, while all users of documents should be concerned with their reliability and validity, the historian has his own conceptual framework and methods of investigation that alert him to the need for caution. The historian is trained to reconstruct past events by reference to their specific place and time. The historian's use of documents is grounded within this context. Social scientists, concerned more with change than with concrete events, use documents more freely. But the absence of reference to a particular time and place and the absence of training in using documents in the social sciences often results in uncritical use. Historians spend lifetimes in establishing the authenticity of documents. Others seize them without thought as convenient grist to their mill.

There are two major difficulties in using existing information in documents. First, the definitions and categories may have been adequate for their original purpose, but not for the social scientist. Second, information in documents may be used as an indicator of a concept, but the fit between them may be dubious. This can be illustrated in criminology where the number of documents relating to offences committed, the nature of the offenders and the disposal of those found guilty suggests a rich fund for research.[3] There are annual reports of the Commissioners of Prisons, the annual report of the Council for Central After-Care Association, the annual report of the Commissioner of Police of the Metropolis, the irregular reports of the Children's Department, Home Office and, above all the *Criminal Statistics for England and Wales* published annually as a blue book six months after the close of the year to which it refers. This seems to be documentary evidence at its most reliable.

Yet this collection of apparent riches cannot even satisfactorily show whether crime is increasing and certainly does not provide an adequate index of existing criminality. This weakness is concealed beneath the deceptive simplicity and certainty of the mass of figures and tables provided. The root of the trouble lies in the initial collection by different groups of person for different purposes using different definitions. *Criminal Statistics* is a collection of reports from chief constables, but these depend on harassed policemen and clerks of courts fitting cases into legally defined categories as best they can.

This legal classification also gives no information about the circumstances of the crime. The weakness in the link between the statistics is in the existence of crimes that are either unknown to the police, ignored by them, or not cleared up. There is no way of knowing how large this figure is compared with those cases that do appear in the statistics. Indeed, an improvement in police efficiency, by reducing this dark figure and inhibiting criminals, may actually reduce the level of crime, but would show in official statistics as a crime wave.

Second, the number of offences in each category depends on current police practice, which is itself influenced by current attitudes towards particular sorts of crime. Sometimes this is a deliberate change in procedure. Thus in 1931 there were 26,000 property offences in the Metropolitan area, but this increased to 83,000 in 1932, because the 'Suspected Stolen Book' was abolished and all cases went into one category.[4] Sometimes discrepancies result from pressures on the police to stamp down on a particular offence. Any such changes in procedure will produce large fluctuations in crime because the offences known to the police are only a small part of the total.

The situation is confused further by the lack of any connection between the three sets of statistics: offences known to the police, persons found guilty in the courts and offences cleared up. Furthermore there is no way of knowing whether the offences were committed by first offenders or hardened criminals. Thus in 1965 there were 292 offences of blackmail cleared up and 179 persons prosecuted. But there was no way of knowing whether these were

179 prosecutions for first offences with the rest cleared up without prosecution, or fewer persons prosecuted for two or more offences and so on.[5]

Moreover, even if these anomalies could be sorted out, the statistics would remain unreliable.[6] Behind criminal statistics are not only overworked clerks doing their best to classify crimes correctly, but a legal system that cannot ensure the proper use of definitions and often aggravates statistical bias by inappropriate definition. The police are reluctant to offend certain prostitutes and homosexuals because they act as important sources of information. The public will not report crimes if they think the law is unfair. Thus prohibition in the United States was almost universally broken.

Above all, criminal statistics give an impression divorced from reality. Policemen have scarce resources. They concentrate these where they seem to be most needed. This usually means concentrating in working-class areas or where business property has to be protected. The police do not usually concern themselves with fiddling of income tax and other white-collar crimes. They are also wary of excessive zeal in pursuing traffic offences which might jeopardise public relations. Within the police system, too, procedures are necessarily arbitrary and imprecise. The author, while station constable in the police, once refused to listen to a woman who complained four times in one week about being assaulted by her boyfriend. The fifth time she encountered a more sympathic ear and action was taken which resulted in a three-year prison sentence for the man concerned. It is on such chances that statistics are built.

To Cicourel, official statistics of juvenile crime are made up in the same way as rumour is generated and transmitted.[7] Vague and discontinuous pieces of information are transformed into ordered occurrences. A written report is prepared that is rounded and simplified to fit the case into the standardised categories of the bureaucratised procedures of justice. A clear picture, not only of the crime, but of the criminal is established through the use of contemporary ideas about causation in delinquency. The police interpret calls, assign men, screen reports, establish routine, label people and fit them into categories. They create histories out of available clues. In doing so they process people into standard types of criminal and, as part of this, into a part of criminal statistics. Bureacracy conceals individuality under statistics and creates convenient fictions of predictability. Thus criminal statistics should not be used as indices of the state of crime but as indices of how delinquents are processed.[8]

From this picture of the processing of delinquents the weakness of criminal statistics can be seen. They represent a simplification into legal categories accomplished through the actions of many hard-pressed officials working according to procedures established within their various offices. But the same process lies behind many apparently neat sets of figures. Furthermore, this process not only applies to statistics compiled by officials, but to those gathered by researchers. To Cicourel the basic question about all information is its relation to the original acts that it represents, indicates or measures. The answers to an interviewer or on a questionnaire, just like the figures in a table of statistics, may not be accurate descriptions of reality, but gross oversimplifications. The researcher uses contemporary theories about delinquency, achievement, ability, opportunities, or environmental influences to shape his report in a form that is convincing to a reader.

To Cicourel the crucial test would be if these interpretations of observations, questionnaires or interviews were defended before an audience who had access to the original documents. He uses the example of an investigator presenting his account of what happened in an event to an audience that had access to video tapes of that event. Immediately the meaning of words, gestures and actions would be in dispute. The policeman, the teacher and the researcher are all engaged in simplifying, objectifying and categorising; the reader only gets their version of the events. It is very likely that access to information that lies behind the written account would produce violent disagreements. Yet such an opportunity is rarely given. Official statistics are usually taken to be reliable indices of the state of actual affairs and the results presented in research reports are rarely accompanied by enough information for the reader to see how the final simplified statistical picture has been produced. All tables and rates conceal and distort reality. Most have been produced by slotting the cases into the nearest category, rather than into one which actually fitted the particular circumstances. In the case of courts, prisons, hospitals, school records, police statistics, government offices and surveys, there are routines for producing the figures in the tables that simplify classification by processing each case into the available categories. The consistent rates that often emerge may be the result of steady, predictable human behaviour. They are as likely to be the result of consistent practices within the organisations producing the figures. It may be, as Cicourel has argued, that the focus of research should be on the labelling and categorising process rather than on the figures themselves.[9]

We can now return to the study of Polish peasants by Thomas and Znaniecki.[10] Not only is this a classic study using the analysis of documents but it has also been subjected to a thorough retrospective evaluation. The authors were concerned with the problems of social change and particularly of immigration. They adopted the viewpoint that such a study, as in all sociology, was necessarily concerned with the way individuals interpreted the situations they were in as well as with the circumstances themselves. Because there was this emphasis on the importance of subjective factors, personal documents were selected as the source of materials for analysis. These were assumed to reveal individual attitudes to events.

The documents used included letters, autobiographies, newspapers, court records and records of social agencies.[11] There was no clear account in the book of the way these materials were obtained. The letters seem to have been bought after an advertisement had been placed in a Polish émigré journal published in North America. The newspapers were bought in Poland by Thomas while on a visit. Documents were collected from an agency concerned with emigration from Poland. There were records from émigré Polish societies in America and court records from areas around Chicago with large Polish populations. Finally there was a long autobiography by a Pole who had only recently left his native land. Blumer, assessing the reliability of these documents as sources from which a picture of changing society could be drawn, concluded that they were inadequate.[12] They were fragmentary, discontinuous, leaving gaps that had to be filled in through the knowledge and imagination of the authors. The letters which formed the bulk of the documentary evidence gave no picture of the background or living conditions of the writers. The picture presented in the book was drawn by the authors, interpreting the material and filling in the gaps from their own knowledge of Polish life. Thomas himself admitted that he and Znaniecki were 'indisputably in the wrong' to give the impression that the theories in the book were founded on data.

This problem of interpretation applied also to the remaining documents. Records of courts or societies, newspapers and life histories had to be interpreted and to Blumer the interpretations that were made were not obvious from the material and in some cases the interpretations that were made were devious and even naïve. Similarly the autobiography could have been interpreted in a number of ways and did not even seem to reflect the genuine views of its author. Furthermore, there was no way in which the reader could judge whether Thomas and Znaniecki's interpretations were correct. All that was clear was that these interpretations were blended together to give a consistent total picture, but one that was drawn by the authors. There was no way of assessing whether this overall picture was valid or whether individual items contributing to it had been interpreted in the way the original author intended.

To Blumer the use of documents as a source of investigating attitudes raises a fundamental dilemma in the social sciences.[13] It is necessary to investigate the meaning people attach to events as well as to study the events themselves. Yet attitudes are elusive things to measure. Personal documents may be indispensable as sources for detecting attitudes, but they do not stand up to the three tests used here. They are open to different interpretations by different readers, they are uncontrolled because they are written freely for non-scientific purposes and they are the work of an individual and therefore not necessarily representative.

Thomas and Znaniecki's study is unique in depending on human documents to develop a theory of social change and in its exposure to critical assessment and defence after a period of twenty years in which it had established itself as a classic. This exercise has served to confirm the difficulties of using documents, even where they are specially written or are contemporary with the events being investigated. There are three sets of interpretations at work to reduce their dependability. The original writer does his best to give meaning to his situation and to communicate his views. The writers who collect and analyse his letter, life history or description then have to write their own account and interpretation. Finally the reader has to decide what this version means. This process may be taken further as later writers use the book or article, interpret and often condense it for another generation of readers. At each stage there is another set of interpretations and further opportunities for introducing bias.

The analysis of documents need not, however, rely on the uncontrolled interpretations of the researcher. There are methods of content analysis that are both objective and systematic. There are explicit rules and procedures that limit the freedom of the researcher to exercise his own judgement over how to categorise and how to decide on what to include or exclude. Thus the reliability of this technique can be high.

Unobtrusive measures

The advantage of documents as sources of evidence is that they have been compiled for other purposes than to provide information for social scientists or historians. They can be assumed to be a reflection of feelings undisturbed by the presence of the researcher. This is also the case with other traces of activity. Humans leave evidence of their activities around, and alert social scientists can use this source to build up a picture of natural behaviour. Webb and others have produced a book on such sources.[14] They range from counting the liquor bottles in dustbins to measuring the wear on carpets in museums.

In practice, unobtrusive measures probably play an important if accidental part in most research. The social scientist going about his everyday activities is alerted to the behaviour of others by the discipline he practises. As he drinks his beer in the pub, squeezes into the tube train or sits in the cinema he takes in the scene with an eye skilled in fitting casual observations into the orderly model in his mind. As he gets involved in planning a research project these models are sensitive to relevant perceptions so that his hunches emerge from a combination of theorising and casual observation.

As interest deepens in a subject alongside the organisation of research, newspapers, journals, radio and TV become sources of information. The researcher interested in curriculum change starts to view school timetables systematically. Those investigating loneliness in old age find new interests in the reading rooms of public libraries, railway station waiting rooms and park seats. Births, marriages and deaths columns in newspapers are perused by those interested in social networks among the middle classes.

Few of these measures are sufficient by themselves to provide reliable data. But they are an important confirmatory source unaffected by the researcher. They can add both insight into and actual measures of human behaviour. Their limitations are those already suggested for all documents, plus the often unsystematic way in which the evidence has accumulated or has to be collected. Nevertheless such measures are probably an important and neglected source of evidence, avoiding many of the snags associated with research involving obtrusion into human activity.

This is an appropriate point at which to close these chapters on research techniques. No single technique is necessarily superior to any other. What is certain is that they all have shortcomings and if used alone are unlikely to give dependable results. This points to the importance of triangulation, the use of multiple methods. The ideal investigation employs a variety of theoretical perspectives, a number of researchers, different research techniques and an assortment of samples. This ensures that the final results will not be the product of one fallible researcher, using one theoretical perspective and one method of data collection. A quick sortie with a questionnaire among students can produce results for rapid publication but equally rapid redundancy. Multiple, cross-checking methods are time-consuming but may have a greater chance of contributing results of lasting value.

TERRORIST OR RESISTANCE FIGHTER? THE CASE OF THE FOOTBALL HOOLIGAN

My contacts with violence on football grounds were divided by the war. My nose was bled at White Hart Lane while unwisely cheering Cliff Bastin as he stroked home a penalty for the great pre-war Arsenal side, and my head was split open by a stray half-brick while spellbound by Benny Fenton at Millwall a decade later. This account of the evidence on football hooliganism is coloured by a personal conviction that life on the terraces has become more peaceful, based on a comparison between Stoke City in the 1970s and London, twenty and thirty years before.

This Controversy should be read as a foreword to Chapter 9. It illustrates the radical nature of ethogenic social science that takes the viewpoint of the subjects of investigation as central, rather than a detached researcher's view of their behaviour. As a consequence, what may be seen as an obvious social problem to the policeman or teacher may be shown to mean something very different to the criminal or pupil. We are in the world of multiple realities. Football hooligans may look like a mindless rabble to seated season ticket holders, but things look different from the terraces, just as it may seem obvious that class 4D are irrational in their disobedience, so 4D may have good reasons for their rejection of the school rules. This controversy over football hooligans is over whether they exist at all as imitators of that troublesome Irish family.

The first major enquiry into football hooliganism was an official report to Denis Howell, then Minister of Sport.[1] This was mainly a questionnaire study. The respondents felt that there was a serious and increasing problem. It led to a working party that suggested many of the crowd control procedures used today. Since the mid-1960s, reports have come in regularly, and most have been based on the assumption that the problem exists and has got worse. Some reports remain at the level of crowd management techniques. Others trace the causes back to declining moral standards generally and to more specific if arguable symptoms of decline such as pop music and violence on television.

It may be however that it is the visibility of the crowd at the popular end, and particularly their audible obscenity that gives the impression of riot. The first reason for caution is spelled out in detail in Chapter 8. It may be that between 1946 and 1960 there were only 195 cases of disorderly behaviour by spectators notified to the Football Association,[2] but the police were rarely in sight and were not particularly interested when I did point out that half-bricks were falling on my head. Between 1960 and 1966 there were 148 cases. But by the end of that period there were more police about, and more cases were probably reported to the F.A. Public interest had been aroused and may have stimulated the rise in numbers in the statistics, through more reporting of incidents and more sympathetic police response.

There is however another possibility that accounts for the crisis on the football grounds. Public interest is both cause and effect of attention by the mass media. The reporters focus on items of popular interest, but also create or increase that interest. The actual incidence of violence in football grounds is low considering the numbers present, their density and the need to create occasional diversions from the boredom of much that occurs on the park. But the press dramatise it. In Hall's terms, they 'edit for impact'.[3] They can stir up 'moral panics'. Last week football violence this week porn in shop windows, next week glue sniffing in primary schools.

When violence on the terraces is investigated by social scientists even more doubt is thrown on the conventional descriptions of mindlessness or thuggery. Taylor[4] sees the fans as the last of the traditional working class supporters, increasingly alienated by the commercialisation of the game and the clubs. The fan is isolated from his team. Clarke[5] also stresses the importance of changes in the 'people's game'. There is a culture of support, passed on from generation to generation which is violated by recent spectacularisation. Close observation of the fans also illuminates an order about their behaviour and in the way new fans are initiated into the terrace organisation.

There are however conflicting aspects in this evidence. If the problem is created by the media, its analysis, and particularly tracing its historical development is pointless. If it doesn't exist it's getting a lot of attention. If it doesn't exist, it is also painful when it draws blood. If it's to do with the alienation of working class youth from a commercialised game, the passion of Manchester's Red Army supporting a side of Irish and Scots recently recruited to replace local lads at the cost of millions is difficult to explain. Furthermore, it seems strange that such effort should have been given to showing that there is an order among the crowd, when you only have to listen to the chanting to realise that there must be a lot of synchronised if vulgar activity.

It is when the research goes beyond describing behaviour on the terraces to accounting for it, that the evidence becomes contradictory. For Taylor and for Clarke, the factors underlying violence lie in the position of working class youth in modern society. The clue to behaviour lies in the erosion of traditional values right at the league footballing heart of that culture. To Taylor, the lad on the terraces '. . . *has the historic task of perpetuating the traditional values of the fast disappearing football subculture . . .*'[6] But to Marsh, 'aggro', with its ritualistic behaviour, is an outlet for natural aggression. ' *Repression of overt expression, coupled with a continued transmission of the aggression process as a central feature of our social fabric*'.[7] But this is not merely a re-run of Controversy 2, where sociological and psychological interpretations were in conflict. Clarke uses the identical historical explanation as Taylor, pointing to the spectacularisation of the game to account for the alienation of the working class fans. From there, Clarke, like Taylor, turns to post-war social conditions. But now it is not a simple reaction against the commercialisation of the game itself, but the physical and social separation of older and younger groups that enables violence to occur, and the need to create excitement and immediacy during the game that accounts for the behaviour behind the goal. Taylor's lads are described as resistance fighters. Marsh sees his boys releasing pent-up aggression, while Clarke sees his football supporters as seeking excitement to compensate for a boring and depressing existence.

As with most of these controversies, there is no way of resolving differences in the analysis of the issue. There are probably elements of all the explanations present, and no doubt many more. In academic courses or discussions, these differences add spice. But when action has to be taken, whether to improve grounds, add to the enjoyment of spectators, including those on the terraces, or keep violence under control, the differences in interpretation do matter, for each leads to different policies. The Joint Sports Council/Social Science Research Council panel on *Public Disorder and Sporting Events*[8] concluded by pointing out several areas where more information was needed, but thought that research had a low priority because it was unlikely to yield much that was useful for action. But Marsh, in a critique of this report, points out that the authors, by searching for solutions, missed the chance of providing a conceptual framework within which recommendations could properly be made. To Marsh, Hall, Clarke and to others interested in the way those on the terraces see the situation, understanding will only come by examining accounts by those involved in the light of the social and political situation in which they find themselves. The dilemma is that while the search for solutions without understanding is futile, there is no agreement among those who claim to understand.

9

INTERPRETATIVE SOCIAL SCIENCE AND ETHNOGRAPHY

So far, the research considered has been 'top down', imposed by the researcher on to the respondents. The researcher has adopted the methods and detached stance of the natural scientist. This involved attempts to control the conditions under which responses have been observed or measured. It meant imposing the stimuli which produced those responses, and the terms in which they were summarised and interpreted. The interest in the respondents has been in their behaviour and its fit into established or anticipated models. The respondent has contributed only reactions to pre-determined stimuli. Even where observation has been used, there has been an emphasis on control over context, timing and incidence. There is clearly a difference between observing an episode, or recording unsolicited statements on one hand, and initiating action by fixing the environment and the action in a laboratory or prearranged group, or asking questions from a schedule, on the other. The first situations allow unforced, spontaneous behaviour to be recorded, the second constrain the action to produce answers to questions determined by the researcher.

Top-down social science, using methods derived from the natural sciences, assumes a similarity between human, social life and the natural world. Yet humans are unsuitable for study by methods designed for studying the unthinking. Humans make sense of their world. They share cultures that include complex languages, spoken and unspoken, that enable intercourse to occur. The imposition of preconstructed categories on social life in order to study it may merely ensure its distortion. In any case, this construction has to be based on everyday, common-sense explanations. What we really need to know are the typical and common ways in which men give meaning to their behaviour, not how they fit into social scientific models of that behaviour, for those models must always be fallible and second hand. This fallibility springs from the paradox that even as a model approached completion and verification through research, it would become part of the social world. It would then be taken into account and the social world would be changed. Thus even if social scientists were successful and social research influential, men would frustrate it. Predictability, the end-product of science, is impossible in the social world. If such a view is held, it seems more sensible to abandon the imitation of natural science and to concentrate on the way humans themselves construct models of the social world as they go about their activity in family, school, football terrace and so on. These everyday models then have to form the basis of a social science.

Bottom-up social science appears under many exotic labels. The various schools have many distinguishing features, but each has such wide variations in practice that their collection together as bottom-up or qualitative perspectives is not excessively simplifying. In sociology, the front runners are social phenomenology and symbolic interactionism. The former has been prominent in the attack on positivism. To Schutz, from whom the rationale for this approach is taken, there is a clear distinction between the scope of natural and social science.[1] The natural scientist can construct, control and define the phenomena he intends to study, because the subject matter is not providing any alternative set of constructions. But the social scientist faces humans who have already interpreted their world, will continue to give it meaning as they are investigated, will also interpret the actions of the researcher, and are capable of coming to their own conclusions about the meaning of events. The social scientist has therefore to find first the way those studied have ordered their world and then translate this into a scientific theory. The latter has to be organised out of the former.

The consequences of adopting this view of social science are profound. The common-sense views of the respondents have to be taken into account and concepts tend to be turned upside down. We have seen this happen with the concepts of delinquency. Instead of being taken as a clearly separate and identifiable category of persons, delinquents were shown to be made by a series of imposed and often arbitrary actions by the law. Thus Young has shown how police action converted a group of hippies who occasionally smoked marihuana into a distinctive group labelled as drug addicts.[2] The labelling produced the effects it was describing. In a similar way, mucking about in schools, violence on the football terraces, fiddling at work, working the system of grades at college, and the nature of academic attainment becomes problematic; not obvious social problems, but issues subject to different perceptions and multiple realities. The best summary is Young's title for his article on the Notting Hill group, 'The Role of the Police as Amplifiers of Delinquency, Negotiators of Reality, and Translators of Fantasy'.[3] To the social phenomenologist, the problem is how groups came to be labelled as deviant, or law-abiding, desirable or devalued, rather than accepting the stereotype and looking for causes and remedies. The social world becomes a much more complicated place and the underworld is seen as a source for explaining what is on the level. The view of the underdog is presented as a counterweight to more conventional studies that take as their starting point the existing balance of power within society. The search for causes ends. The social world is seen as negotiated by interacting humans, not determined by detectable laws.

Typical of this approach are studies of the hidden economy. Economists have not only a poor record in predicting economic trends and in recommending solutions to economic woes, but often seem to be concerned with a fictional business scene. While moonlighting, fixed overtime, tax fiddling and fringe benefits are of major concern to those actually on the job, economists focus exclusively on the surface of events. But there have always been social scientists concerned with the way workers improve their conditions, supplement their wage packets and avoid paying taxes. These studies are important, not only because they describe actual working arrangements rather than fictionalised accounts, but because trade unions, employers, quangos and other organisations concerned with modern economies, increasingly control events without reference to law or to government. The large multi-national corporation has a hidden economy as has the dock worker or bread roundsman.

Studies of the hidden economy also have to be clandestine. Henry becomes a driver, cellarman and sales assistant for a wines and spirits merchant.[4] Ditton becomes a bread salesman[5] and Mars makes himself at home around the docks.[6] Each observes the way workers fiddle and pilfer. When Henry interviews he tape-records so that verbatim statements can be included in the written report. These studies are in the anthropological tradition. Only when the social networks come to be known can the extent of the hidden economy among them be appreciated. Some fiddling can bring immediate profit. But traffic in goods requires trading networks. A society of unofficial wholesalers becomes visible.

There is a tendency to see fiddling as inevitable in those studies. The observations are concentrated on the dishonest and the remainder get few mentions. Indeed, the impression is of a crooked world in which the honest are deviant. But this is the punch behind these studies. They are not only of the underworld, but show how this extends through normal social relations. By detecting what is going on below the surface, the surface can be understood. Multiple realities really become real. This focus on the hidden, and generalisation to the visible, is a valuable antidote to the more conventional top-down view that has dominated social science. But the focus inevitably involves selectivity. The observations can prove overwhelming and sifting among them to find common elements can easily lead to bias. The reader should look for checks on the way selection has been made among the data collected, or at least ensure that the researcher was aware that there was a problem as he used his tapes and field notes. Fletcher has provided a despairing but insightful account of the qualitative researcher's dilemma.[7] Researchers are liable to feel drowned amid the accumulated subtleties of human behaviour.

The methods used in research approached from a symbolic interaction perspective have to uncover the meanings of those involved.[8] Accepting the unity of theories and methods, Denzin argues that a book on methods from a functionalist perspective would differ from one written from some other theoretical position. His own preference for symbolic interactionism leads him to concentrate on both the interaction and the symbols, or meanings, that are given to explain the interaction from the actor's point of view. The sociologist has to operate in two worlds. First, there is the sociologist's conceptions of the behaviour of those he is studying. Second, there are the motives and definitions that the subject gives to his own behaviour. To Becker, the sociological view of the world is *'abstract, relativistic and generalising'*.[9] Marihuana users do not use terms such as rationalisation, socialisation and role behaviour. They use everyday concepts that tend to be concrete and specific to the situation. Sociologists add the abstract, generalised terms.

This separation of scientific and everyday conceptions leads to the key difference between the methods borrowed from the natural sciences and those adopted by interpretative social scientists. In the former, the social scientist initiates responses and then interprets them within previously determined, scientific frames of reference. In the latter the social scientist first learns about the everyday conceptions of the natural situation from those involved and then interprets them. In practice the difference may not be great between the two approaches. Positivist social scientists often carry out exploratory pilot studies, combine participant observation with more structured methods and include open-ended questions in their schedules. Interpretative social scientists also use predetermined interviews and questions. They may try to get inside the everyday conceptions of those investigated without any preconceptions, but it is likely that these will influence perception. The difference remains important, however. Researchers do experiment, or survey, without taking notice of the everyday, common-sense definitions of the subjects being taken into account. Others only report the verbatim accounts collected from respondents. The different theoretical positions include different methods.

Symbolic interactionism is concerned with the way humans interpret their own conduct, and that of others, as they interact. The action undertaken is seen as self-conscious and pragmatic. The meanings of events are continually subject to re-negotiation. The implications for social research were profound.[10] The focus should be on the actor and the way he perceives, interprets and assesses the social world around him. The conventional researcher's role of detached observer is useless. The appropriate position for research is from the actor's viewpoint. The researcher has to take on the role of the actor. To remain detached, to attempt to preserve objectivity, means imposing on the actor's own perceptions and consequently ensuring their distortion. Symbolic interactionism reverses the role of the researcher. Mead's work kept the study of small groups active. Through Herbert Blumer it remained influential until the 1960s, when many social scientists abandoned the more conventional, natural science research stance and adopted some combination of social phenomenology and symbolic interactionism as a guide to their investigations.[11]

In Britain, the social phenomenological approach has been most influential through the Open University's *School and Society* course[12] and through M. F. D. Young's collection of readings in *Knowledge and Control: New Directions for the Sociology of Education*.[13] These works turned the sociology of education upside down and have been followed by a series of books reporting mainly small-scale studies of life in classrooms. Significantly, the major influences in this movement in Britain, Bernstein and M. F. D. Young, have continued to take the main concern of the sociology of education to be the relation between the way knowledge is organised in schools and the way social control is exercised in society. But the publication of *Knowledge and Control* focused attention on the curriculum of schools and what was going on in classrooms. The empirically based articles in this book retained the interest in the relation between social control within and around the school, but the wave of research that was sparked off by it tended to lose the wider focus, or to tack it on as a concluding section. The conceptualisation of much of the work narrowed to include only school processes rather than the relation between the curriculum, the life of the children outside the school and the economic, political and social structure.

The reader is in a difficult position in assessing the basis in evidence of the 'new' sociology of education. Thus both Esland's[14] and Keddie's[15] essays in *Knowledge and Control* are based on studies in schools. But only the sketchiest details are given of this work and there is no way in which its credibility can be assessed. This is unfortunate given the message of these authors. Esland, for example is suggesting that knowledge is a human product and that validity is an ideological position. What is true is decided by the ability of interests to secure their case. Thus knowledge is seen as valid if it suits the interests of those in a position to decide what should be taught and valued. If such views are held there is little point in agonising over reliability or validity. Research and evidence are part of the apparatus for sustaining cultural hegemony and are inseparable from other forms of propaganda. Indeed, from this view there is little point in a social science as all knowledge has only relative credibility. What is valid depends on whether you are in the driving seat or being driven.

Bernbaum, in a detailed analysis of developments within the sociology of education, rejects the criticism of the 1950s work linking educational opportunity and social class as taking problems for the system rather than taking the system itself as problematic.[16] To him the sociologists of the 1950s and early 1960s were not supporting the existing system, but determined to get it changed by producing evidence of its unfairness. But there is a crucial difference between the old and the new. Writers like Floud and Halsey were committed to the possibility of arriving at the truth. In their work it is possible to explore the tension between ideology and evidence. More recent work lacks this commitment and leaves the reader with no possibility of deciding on the possibility of objectivity. This is an affirmation of the importance of criteria for assessing the validity of evidence and of giving the reader enough information to allow him to see how far they have been satisfied. The four key questions in the foreword of this book are in the positivist tradition, but they give the reader a chance of determining credibility. Researchers can easily conceal weaknesses in design and in results, but the commitment to giving information on the way evidence has been collected is an acknowledgement of the possibility of producing dependable evidence.

In social psychology, Hargreaves's, working mainly within the symbolic interactionist tradition, has been another important influence within British education. His *Social Relations in a Secondary School*[17] was the first detailed study of the effects of streaming to be published. It is a study of the relations between teachers and pupils, and among the latter. It was an arresting study because it produced the first British account of schooling from the viewpoint of the pupils. The focus on delinquent sub-cultures within the school has continued in Hargreaves's work. *Deviance in Classrooms*[18] published in 1975 with Hestor and Mellor, looks specifically at the way rules are generated in the classroom and deviance attributed to pupils. This work is placed explicitly in the social phenomenological camp. It examines the applicability of labelling theory to schools. Like most of the work in this area it combines insights from social phenomenology and symbolic interactionism.

The problem with *Deviance in Classrooms* for the reader is that much has to be taken on trust. Hargreaves's track record in research and his consistently insightful writing on interpersonal relations are a source of security. The book smacks of validity. It rings true to anyone who has taught in the non-selective school sector. But this pupil's-eye view of the school world raises problems. The object is to bring on to the printed page the world of the pupils and of the teachers. There can be no departure from this objective, for that would be to impose the concepts of the researchers on to the actors. But how can the reader tell whether it is a faithful reproduction, rather than a reconstruction through the models referred to, consciously or not, by the researchers? This is an impossible question to answer. It is a re-phrasing of the question on reliability, but in this case any weakness undermines the theoretical position from which the researchers start. Yet there is no description in the book of the methods used beyond the reasons for picking the two schools involved. The authors write that they will make every effort to report self-consciously on the relation between their investigative work and the subject of their investigation, because of the approach they are using. But the reader is still left to guess how the information was collected, how the researchers controlled their own influence within the classrooms and how the context of the work may have affected the data obtained.

The problem for the reader is even more acute in other studies of this kind. For example, Marsh, Rosser and Harré, in their book *The Rules of Disorder*,[19] produce a study 'Trouble in School' that is very similar to that of Hargreaves, Hestor and Mellor in looking at the way pupils and teachers interact. Here however there is no prevarication. The school is seen as the type that has not adapted itself to alternative, non-academic needs and which, in general, is not sensitive to the fact that pupils are people with as much right as anyone else to be respected. The pupils were seen to be seeking to establish their power within the classrooms to counterbalance perceived affronts to their dignity. Now this may be true and unquestionably does happen. But there is no way of telling from the information provided in this account. Indeed, while the insensitivity of the teachers is reported as half the problem, there are no accounts of the teachers' views as there are of the pupils. There is also no indication of checks being made on the accounts given by these pupils. If they felt devalued by the teachers and that their dignity was being affronted, how did they feel about these academics being around the school? Some of the accounts suggest some rather curious questions from the researchers, but these are not included. The reader is left to guess how the passages included were selected. There is not even any detail on the number of visits to the school, on its organisation and environment nor of the relations with the staff.

This study, as with most of these classroom investigations, covers relations between teachers and pupils, but does not include anything from the former. The difficulty may be partly teacher reluctance to contribute. It is partly that the interest is in the underdog view. But the omission is, particularly in the light of the theoretical position taken, reprehensible. It is similar to the failure to include accounts from the police alongside those of delinquents when discussing labelling. But this omission is part of a wider neglect of the issue of reliability. It is possible to collect accounts from participants in different positions and check them to see if there are discrepancies. It is possible to check accounts from the same person at different times. There are great difficulties in interpreting audio and video tapes. It is the unspoken and not only the words that give the message. Responses are influenced by the researcher and the subject of the research. Some check is necessary and those checks need to be reported to the reader. If they are not, scepticism is appropriate. Researchers are guilty of unreliability until proved innocent.

Accounting for behaviour, looking for the way men give meanings to their interactions and try to understand the social world around them, has been a continuing tradition within sociology, through the influence of the Chicago School of Sociology which was the major producer of graduate sociologists in the United States before the Second World War.[20] Interpretative approaches to human interaction have had less influence within psychology itself. Here the emphasis on observing and measuring behaviour, and the experimental method, has remained dominant. However there has been a recent surge of interest in studying humans as planning, reasoning persons capable of giving valid accounts of interactions. This approach, recommended by Harré and Secord in their book *The Explanation of Social Behaviour*, was labelled by them 'ethogenic'.[21]

The change from looking at human responses to stimuli in the laboratory, to recording their theories about the situations they find themselves in, is radical within psychology, although this approach has been sustained within sociology for over half a century. To Harré, humans use models of the social world, of social order, of social class, of family, of other ethnic groups and so on, to organise their behaviour.[22] The task of the researcher is to study these models through the accounts that those who use them are capable of giving. The social world is seen as a series of episodes wherein individuals employing their own models of the world, interact. That interaction is possible because there is correspondence between the models employed. Interaction takes place because it is given meaning by those involved. These meanings are common-sense understandings of the social world and are the focus for ethogenic research.

The similarity between this approach and interpretative sociology is obvious. The subject studied, such as football hooligans and classroom miscreants, are also similar. All such research depends on the recording of accounts by participants. Cross-checking methods can be used to confirm that the accounts are authentic, although such studies as Marsh, Rosser and Harré's *Rules of Disorder* do not employ them.[23] The crucial area of the research is in the analysis of speech and the interpretation of what has been said. The researcher's report is an account of the accounts given by those investigated. But the researcher has to interpret what has been said in order to produce his summary. He is looking for common features among the individual accounts. For the reader, this is the area to question. Do these individual accounts, these verbatim statements, add up to the interpretation given by the researcher?

To answer this question on the credence that can be given to the researcher's account of accounts, let us return to the football terraces. Appropriately dressed, our researcher mingles with the crowd. He gets the flavour of the scene and eventually feels confident enough to start asking questions. Where is he to start?

Producing a tape recorder on the terraces may be possible but dangerous. The club may cooperate and allow a long-focus camera to be used. But eventually he will have to ask questions in a less noisy place. This placement, the acceptability of the researcher, the flavour of the questions, the nearness of other supporters, and all the factors making up the context of the accounting, matter. Pupils interviewed in the deputy head's study give very different responses to the same questions as pupils interviewed in the playground or in their own rooms in their own homes. Adults are adults if they are sociologists, and are fair game for the leg-pulling answer.

The reader has also to concentrate on the way the researcher interprets the accounts. Reference back to the trauma of transition or to the capitalist class structure have been shown to produce very different interpretations in studies of school leavers. Similarly, discrepancies have been illustrated among studies of football supporters. Every researcher faces a problem when he tries to interpret data. But in ethogenic research the problem is exacerbated. The object is to report the views of the respondents, not to impose the researcher's view. Yet the latter inevitably enter when the total scene is being interpreted and may pervade the selection of accounts and even their content.

There are ways around this problem which have rarely been exploited. The data could be given to those involved for interpretation. Teachers for example could interpret the recordings made of pupils and a summary account by teachers reported alongside that of the researcher. In a similar way, pupils could be used to interpret accounts of their accounts or those of their teachers. If the accounts of those involved are valid, there is no reason why their summary of accounts should not be valid. This is the world of multiple realities, of different perceptions. The perception of the situation by other groups involved would counterbalance any bias inserted by the researcher. Alternatively, the researcher could present his report to the parties involved and include their comments in his article or book. The author did this in a study of a curriculum development project and readers found the inserted comments more revealing than the account itself.[24] Certainly I never appreciated how obtrusive I had been until I received comments from the project team. These comments were included in the book reporting this research and served as a useful caution to my claims to be a detached observer.

The hero of the ethogenic school is Erving Goffman.[25] Goffman is primarily concerned with the human capacity for controlling the presentation of self to others through monitoring the way others control their own performances. To Goffman, humans are like actors adjusting their performance to present a role to the audience through their ability to read the responses of that audience. Here is the rational, self-monitoring individual conceived as the basis for a new ethogenic approach to psychology. Significantly Goffman has long been a hero to qualitative, interpretive sociologists.

Goffman's similes of the drama have dangers. The analogy between life and the stage can be stretched too far. Man may be continually concerned with the management of the impressions that he gives to others, but as Garfinkel[26] has pointed out, a world peopled with Goffman-type members would be incongruous. It is difficult to see how social life could continue if we were all managing our impressions as actors on the stage. Somewhere, sometime, someone has to act in a candid fashion for anything to get done, just as there has to be a surface economy for there to be one hidden. Goffman busies away in small-scale action and has produced a flow of entertaining and illuminating similes. But similes they remain. We may act out a 'line' in social encounters, and assume that others we meet are doing so. We may act out 'performances', cooperate in 'teams' over those 'performances', have the opportunity of playing 'discrepant roles' if we don't want to play with the 'team', engage in 'face' rituals to save our prestige and play a variety of 'games' to secure our own ends. But these insights are derived from small scale interactions. They are mini-sociology. There is no easy way in which they can contribute to a social science concerned with power, the distribution of wealth, income and opportunities, with social change or with the reality of revolution. To Gouldner,[27] the whole dramaturgical enterprise is trivialising social science and his attack on Goffman is one of the most swingeing in a subject not noted for its civility.

The immediate danger for the reader in authors such as Goffman is seduction. It all seems very plausible, it is clearly illuminating. All the world is indeed a stage upon which we play. When we read about it in studies of hotels, or restaurants, or asylums, it is a revelation. But the question on reliability is an antidote. Would another researcher really detect the same interactions using Goffman's methods? It is unlikely, but as no methods are included in Goffman's work it is useless to speculate. There is no idea given of the way the insights are obtained. There may be fieldwork, but not even this is sure in some cases.

Ethnography and the anthropological tradition

The ethnographic method, wherein the social customs of groups are studied on the ground, has a long history and is particularly suited to the symbolic interaction approach where the focus is on the meaning of events. It is the method of anthropology. As early as 1922, Malinowski had outlined the method of participant observation,[28] and in 1928, Thrasher outlined how he had used the same method in his study of gangs in Chicago.[29] There is a direct line to studies such as Willis's *Profane Culture* published in 1978[30] and based on an ethnographic study of a group of hippies and a group of motor-bike enthusiasts. These studies share a method. The interpretation of the data collected is made by reference to very different theoretical positions.

Studies such as James Patrick's *A Glasgow Gang Observed*[31] are direct descendents of classic studies such as Whyte's *Street Corner Society*,[32] to the Chicago School of Sociology and to writers like Thrasher on gangs, Anderson on hobos[33] and Shaw on jack rollers.[34] Another fertile tradition has been the studies of the 'hidden economy' of fiddling.[35] These ethnographic studies have also proved to be a rich vein within education where the study of classroom interaction blossomed in the 1970s. All these studies provide insights into human interaction. They ring true because they are descriptive. They merge into good journalism and are separable from it through the pre-specification of methods used, the control exercised during use and the criteria laid down for accepting evidence as valid. Once again, the reader has to look very carefully at the passages describing the methods used. Where none exists it is safest to assume that it is journalistic, informed by a sociological or psychological perspective.

The ethnographic method is also used to collect data which is explicitly interpreted within a theoretical context. For example, many of these research reports are interpreted within a Marxist framework. There is no attempt to conceal this from the reader, although it is rarely spelled out in detail. The various forms of Marxism are respectable and established academic frameworks for interpreting such data which lends itself to analysis within any available model. In these cases the work is safest considered as two parts. First there is the data itself, then its interpretation. For example, *Learning to Labour* by Willis,[36] or the same author's *Profane Culture*[37] are full of observations that grip. The sexist, racialist views, the acceptance of work ethic and its intimate connection with masculinity, and the arrogance and even confidence of these working class adolescents are vividly reported. In *Learning to Labour* the adoption of such views is shown to be a form of self-condemnation. It explains how working class lads get working class jobs. The reference is to the capitalist class system. But there are no references to social class, to alienation, to hegemony, to the other concepts used in the analysis within the first, descriptive part, largely contributed by those studied. The second part is only loosely derived from the first and in parts seems to contradict it. As Musgrove has pointed out in a review of *Profane Culture*, the groups studied are first described as apolitical, unaware of class oppression and exploitation, and then interpreted as selecting, developing and transforming their environment to make their own distinctive culture.[38] In one part they are seen as unconcerned with the institutional structure of society and in the second as concerned with transforming it. It is inconsistent to support a method that denies the validity of imposing a predetermined structure on those observed, but to impose such a structure on their accounts. There has to be an account of accounts, but the reality of the actor has to be respected from start to finish. The problem with ethnography is that the meanings of those involved are explained by the researcher in a way that makes the key questions in the Foreword to this book very difficult to answer.

Combining perspectives, techniques, data and interpretations

In Chapters 4 to 9 and in the controversies that preceded each chapter, the solidity of evidence has been probed. Much of the disagreement arose from the different theoretical position taken by the researchers. In other cases different methods have produced different types of data. Even within a single social science there are many distinct perspectives, only some of which have been examined in this chapter. The close relation between methods of investigation and the theories that provide their rationale ensures that the evidence produced will reflect different aspects of the issues investigated, and different interpretations of similar data.

This variety within each of the social sciences has the advantage of presenting the reader with a number of perspectives, and the chance of deciding the priorities which they should be accorded. It is hoped that this book will promote the discrimination that is required. It also gives the social researcher a number of possible approaches to any subject which he wishes to investigate. Few social scientists take an eclectic view. Most hold very strongly to one theoretical position and this determines the methods they prefer. However, there are obvious limitations and dangers of bias in a study that is carried out by a single researcher, from one distinctive theoretical position, using one method only. Indeed, Denzin has argued that the social world studied by sociologists consists of definitions, attitudes and personal values. Each social researcher will concentrate on different aspects of this confused reality. As a consequence each will decide that different methods are appropriate. Thus Denzin supports triangulation, the use of multiple approaches to study the same object.

Triangulation of methods is common. Each method has its strengths. For example, in studies of schools, researchers such as Hargreaves[39] or Lacey[40] rely heavily on observation because activity is left undisturbed. But there is no way of observing more than a few critical events. Thus pupils and teachers are interviewed, questionnaires used and school records examined. Where a single method is used the reader should envisage the complicated social situation that the evidence is supposed to reflect. Gabriel's teachers who returned the postal questionnaire on their emotional problems in the classroom were having to condense their experiences into answers to questions that may have had little relevance.[41] Hemming's adolescent girls writing to a weekly journal might not have been absolutely honest about their problems.[42] Where one method only has been used there is a one-dimensional snapshot of a very wide and deep social scene.

Triangulation can also be applied to the data itself. It can be collected from different samples, at different times, in different places. This is obviously time-consuming, but reduces the chance of one-sided evidence. Marsh, Rosser and Harré in *Rules of Disorder* examine pupil–teacher interaction, but do not give any accounts by teachers.[43] School classes observed on Friday afternoons will look different on Tuesday morning. The differences between the school leavers in the studies by Willis and by Scharff reported in Controversy 2 may have resulted from the place where the interview took place. The spectre of one deputy head in a West Midlands secondary modern school pervaded several classrooms in one school investigated by the author in the early 1960s.[44] In these classrooms there was peace. Elsewhere the same classes became roaring boys.

Denzin has also argued that more than one observer should be used.[45] This does not mean that the work should be sub-contracted to as many assistants as can be hired. Denzin is arguing for the authors of the research to be involved so that their observations can cross-check. He also recommends multiple theoretical perspectives, so that different interpretations of the same data will be made public. Such triangulation would be expensive and beyond most of the researchers whose work is reported in this book. Yet such cross-checking can be built into the most modest of work. The confidence of the reader in the work depends on such triangulation. If it is not built into a single account, then comparisons with other research in the same area should be made. Here the introductory and concluding sections of any report of research should be examined. Confirmations and refutations from other work should be reported, and discrepancies examined. Such an examination introduces a form of retrospective triangulation.

One spin-off from triangulation is an increase in the chances of reconciling different theoretical positions. This means that research can help to improve the quality of the theory that guides it. But there is another, more practical possibility. The data collected, or the interpretations given it in reports or books, can be triangulated by those around the scene. It will be argued later that there are many administrators, inspectors, teachers, social workers and so on who are in a good position to bring to bear another perspective on evidence collected. Once again this would increase the confidence of the reader that the account was balanced, or would allow him to judge between different interpretations. This is accepting the whole logic of triangulation. It is an admission that the complexity of social life requires a variety of research approaches. But researchers are often not the only ones producing evidence. They are certainly not the only ones capable of interpreting it.

THE PRIORITY GIVEN TO REDUCING THE SIZE OF SCHOOL CLASSES

In moving to three final chapters which deal with the presentation and use of evidence, it is instructive to look at a controversy where researchers seem to oppose current priorities in education and, indeed, apparent common sense. Fleming in 1959,[1] Rossi in 1970[2] and Powell in 1978,[3] reviewing the available studies, which by the 1970s ran into hundreds, all concluded that the findings were not conclusive, but that if there was any relation, it was that large classes tended to contain children whose attainment in basic skills was higher than that of their apparently more fortunate peers in smaller classes.

Four recent studies have confirmed that the only measurable difference favours large classes as environments for learning. A large-scale study of achievement in mathematics carried out in ten countries and covering 132,775 pupils and 19,000 teachers found no apparent connection between class size and the level of mathematics achieved.[4] What indications there were suggested that countries with larger classes got better results. A study in London by Little and Russell found that children in large classes learned to read faster.[5] Morris, in a study for the National Foundation for Educational Research involving 8,197 pupils in sixty Kent primary schools, found that reading standards were better on average in larger classes.[6] Finally, Davie using material from the National Child Development Study came to similar conclusions.[7] Here 92 per cent of the 17,000 children born in one week in 1958 were traced in 1965 and given a number of tests. The information gathered on their infant schooling showed that those in classes over forty-one tended to do better than those in classes of under thirty on the tests of reading, arithmetic and social

150   *The Limitations of Social Research*

adjustment.

There may of course be very good reasons why measured attainment appears to be higher in larger classes. Poor attainers may be placed in small groups for remedial purposes. The best teachers may be placed with larger groups. Larger classes may be in popular schools, attracting more motivated children. Larger classes may necessitate formal teaching methods which lead to superior test scores, although broader aspects of learning may be neglected. The real benefits of smaller classes may come around twenty or fifteen or under, not around twenty-five when compared with thirty or thirty-five. Teachers in small classes may be using informal methods that require a level of skill that is beyond many. However, many of these factors can be controlled. Burstall however has pointed out that small-scale studies containing observations in classrooms suggest, as with the streaming versus non-streaming controversy, that teachers' attitude may be important.[8] Teachers did not seem to adjust their style to smaller classes when the opportunity to do so arose, even though they believed that they had done so. These small-scale studies also tend to show higher attainment with smaller classes. Burstall suggests that this may be due to the discontent of teachers taking large classes. Thus class size by itself may be a minor issue. The important one is the effectiveness of teaching styles in relation to the aims of the teachers, and to the conditions, including the size of class, that is the context of their work.

However, the evidence remains embarrassing when the reduction of class sizes has such a high priority. In the Plowden Report the Committee was faced with their own survey that came up with the usual result that large classes seem to facilitate greater achievement.[9] Yet their conclusion was that reduction in class size should remain a priority. The means for reconciling this are illuminating. The researchers reluctantly confirmed their unfortunate findings despite their efforts to eliminate them through control over possible spurious factors. The Report mentions the results, but says these are outweighed by professional advice, public opinion and the example of other countries. The writers of the Report seemed to have used evidence only where it supported their views and explained it away where it opposed them. Part 1 of the Report seemed to bear no connection to the evidence in Part 2.

Davie and other researchers have stressed that there are reasons for reducing the size of classes other than to increase attainment. However, the evidence does make the high priority given to such a reduction suspect at a time of shortage of funds. Given the mass of evidence on the adverse effect of poor environment on attainment there is a good case for improving education by better housing, welfare services and pre-school education rather than training more teachers and building more classrooms. But this is heresy, even though the evidence that is available seems to support such a redistribution of scarce resources.

10

THE PREPARATION AND PRESENTATION OF EVIDENCE

The emphasis in this book on the importance of scientific communities in determining what counts as valid evidence is part of a wider aspect of modern scientific activity. It is conventionally communal and public rather than individual and clandestine. The alchemist produced many of the ideas and techniques of early chemistry. But chemistry took off only when methods and results were shared rather then hidden in the hope of personal gain. Scientists remain motivated by the hope that they will be first to a discovery. Until the breakthrough is made it is kept within the research group. But to get a Nobel prize or the respect of colleagues requires publication. The work will only be accepted if peers accept the account to be reliable and valid. This will only be accorded if there is sufficient evidence published for them to be certain.

There is of course much science, in industry, for government and by research institutes, that is confidential. There are other areas where the capital employed is so large that no replication is possible. Nevertheless, modern natural science is no longer a private activity. The big breakthrough tends to require big resources and large support staffs. The national and international communities scrutinise new evidence in the light of closely related work.

In social science, the private, one-person researcher remains active at the centre of university-based research. The communities exist, but tend to be loose-knit, to lack journals which specialise in quick publication of research results, and to fission and re-form frequently. This allows the merchant adventurer and the swash-buckler to flourish. Much of the best work is done by the lone

Ph.D. student. The informed amateur is not excluded either by the capital required for research, or the exclusiveness of the scientific communities. Evidence is often prepared in private and presented without reference to others working in the relevant area. There are great advantages in this scope for enterprise, particularly given the major role of social science in exposing the gap between ideal and reality. But it does increase the need for caution by the reader. That caution is however necessary in assessing all evidence. So far the stages from conceptualisation to data collection have been covered. Now the preparation of evidence for publication is considered.

The human hand in the advanced technology

There is a significant parallel between the organisation of technically advanced, urban, industrial societies and the production of sophisticated statistics on the way people live within them. The nineteenth century statistical societies and the 1980s social surveys examine similar phenomena for similar purposes. The techniques have been improved. But improvements in sampling have not eliminated unrepresentative samples. Designs and techniques still depend on human interpretation and accuracy. The easiest way of illustrating this is to examine the effects of computers on data processing. Anyone who has watched a line-printer or visual display output from a computer is liable to lose sight of the many stages where human error can have affected the figures.

The data that arrives back from the field after a survey or experiment has to be translated from answers to numbers for statistical analysis by the computer. There will already be problems over sampling, response, poor questions, interviewer bias and so on, making the data, or lack of some of it, an incomplete or misleading picture. But the words now have to be converted into punched slots on one of the columns on an IBM card, or punched directly on to a computer tape or disc. Now there is no problem over many answers. Male or female is either coded 1 or 2. Age is slightly more difficult, for there are only 80 columns for 80 answers on each card and space can rarely be afforded so that each year can be punched in. Occupation is even more difficult. Nevertheless instructions on how to code the various responses are not too difficult with such easily structured questions.

The real problem comes where the answers are numerous or unpredictable. It is not always possible to pre-code, to decide on the number that is to be given all predicted answers. Even where this is attempted there will be answers that do not fit. Someone has to decide on the coding of answers and someone has to do the job. There are inevitably arbitrary decisions in grouping varied answers together so that they are given the same code number. The researcher is imposing categories on responses. It has been repeatedly stressed that this imposition is a major criticism of social scientific research. It is another stage where responses are being interpreted and transformed.

When decisions have been made about the numbers to be given to responses, the schedules are ready for coding. This can be done by the researchers, or by assistants after a little training. But it is a monotonous job and errors happen. These are likely to cancel out with no harm done. But clerical coders may not consult over tricky cases and may code according to their interpretation. They may not have fully understood the instructions. Errors resulting from such sources are liable to be systematic and distorting. Where the researcher does the job, the scope of interpretations that will lead to the results anticipated is ever-present. The computer can be programmed to edit the data fed into it, but this cross-checking to detect mistakes can not cover all items. In many cases the 'garbage in, garbage out' rule for computers will apply. The technology can not cover for all human error, and those that can not be covered are likely to be important.

Coding is not the only stage between data collection and computer output where errors can be made. Once the coded data sheets are prepared they go for punching, usually outside the control of the researcher. Punch operators also make mistakes and these may not cancel out. Meanwhile, in programming to process the previously prepared data more human errors may be built in. The big cases, where the quarterly electricity bill runs into thousands of pounds, receive publicity. But all the researchers are on the lookout for such mistakes as they look through their printouts.

The persistence of human hands in modern technology means

that readers should not be seduced by sophistication. The computer can churn out figures from the most fragile data. It can obscure gross weaknesses. If average scores of a school class are compared on two occasions, one when a bright child was absent and the other when the absentee was less able, no amount of sophistication will remedy the original error. If engineers are all coded as working class or all women coded according to their husband's occupation, the consequences will persist through analysis into results. Computerisation can not compensate for bias or for mistakes made in earlier stages of research.

Statistics as a prop

A comparison between government reports or private enquiries of today with those 150 years ago shows how far we have moved into an age of statistics. Education reports before 1950 contained few figures or tables. None was based on systematic bespoke research. It is now common to publish major reports in two parts, one a report, the other a tabulation of statistical data. But the apparently uncontroversial official statistics are produced to support particular policies and to inform the machinery of government. Some critics see the sinister side of this. Miles and Irvine for example[1] state that 'Behind the veil of neutrality, official statistics thus form part of the process of maintaining and reproducing the dominant ideologies of capitalist society.' The statistics also reflect curious balances in concern over majority and minority concerns. Thus the Newsom Report, *Half Our Future*, contained fifteen pages on the accompanying survey, while the Robbins report on higher education contained 2,097 pages of evidence published in separate volumes.[2]

The mass of supporting statistics in contemporary reports is the swollen descendant of the efforts of the Benthamites in the 1830s to produce hard information on which to base new policies to cure new urban, industrial problems. The pioneer efforts of statistical societies in London and Manchester, of medical officers of health, of officials like Chadwick or of energetic citizens like Engels or Booth have blossomed into the principle that every opinion needs its reinforcement of figures to appear respectable. Simple, even non-mathematical, texts abound.[3] There are also others detailing mistakes in the presentation.[4] There are even articles to help researchers to boost the appearance of reliability of their work.[5]

The need for caution over statistical presentation is illustrated in the use of the term 'significance' and the use of significance levels. It is very impressive to read that the results are significant at the 1 or 5 per cent level. But this figure only indicates the possibility that the statistics presented have occurred through chance rather than through the existence of some genuine difference or association. The chance refers to the sample used. The 1 per cent level of significance means that there is only one chance in a hundred that the results were due to the particular sample that was used.

However, many writers have argued that significance tests are used in situations where they are inappropriate or even misleading. Labovitz, reviewing the evidence available to 1970, concluded that significance tests are not useful in social research and should be disregarded when they appear.[6] Writers on the use of such tests did not agree on areas where they were legitimate. Nine papers supported their use only where random sampling had been used. But Gold has argued that genuine random sampling is impossible.[7] Selvin's view is that they should be confined to experimental studies.[8] Similarly Coleman has argued that they are misleading in survey studies because they only give a measure of the possibility that results are due to chance whereas other factors may exist that would provide a better guide.[9] Camilleri maintains that they should only be used to test theories but not specific hypotheses.[10] There is no agreement. Uses seen as legitimate by one writer are rejected by others.

The persistence of significance tests in social research in the face of such criticisms can be explained first by their apparent precision. Indeed, their use may actually obscure the presence of uncontrolled extraneous variables and accumulated bias. The tests have become an important convention of social science and every higher degree student feels the need to find room for some somewhere in his thesis. They give an appearance of certainty associated with the natural sciences. Above all they impress on the outsider and amateur the superiority of social science as a source of wisdom about important topical issues.

Words as window dressing

The object of writing an account of research is to convey information with precision. If the readers are not fellow professionals this also requires the use of plain words. Yet economics, psychology and sociology were given by Gowers as examples of new disciplines using jargon.[11] The tendency of writers in the social sciences to be 'jargantuan' is unfortunate, as these disciplines owe their expansion to their apparent relevance to problems that concern the lay public. But the real danger is that the use of complicated words, whether accidentally or intentionally, can attach a veneer of academic superiority to inferior material. A technical vocabulary is necessary for clarity and precision of meaning, but can also serve as a smokescreen.

The disasters are reports worded like the 'Development of Educational Theory Derived from Three Educational Theory Models' submitted to the US Office of Education, containing the information that 'Storeputness is a system with inputness that is not fromputness'.[12] The likely response to jargon can be gauged from the attitudes of teachers to research. Cane and Schroeder have shown how sensitive and annoyed teachers are with technical terms.[13] Southgate and Roberts, in a book to help teachers over the criteria for choosing a method of teaching reading, comment that none of the research has been reported in a manner that would allow teachers to comprehend and interpret it in the context of their jobs in the classroom.[14] Yet teachers are an educated minority interested in obtaining guidance from research evidence.

The problem becomes apparent when examination papers are marked. Thus the work of Bernstein on language has produced a mass of misunderstandings and howlers. The belief that working-class children are linguistically all depraved, converse only in monosyllables and grunts, and never speak to their parents, while middle-class children are continually employing elaborate 'sinta-xis' in philosophical family discussions, springs from a desperate attempt to understand and reproduce this sophisticated theory. The alternatives are to use original articles written in an unbending difficult style or rely on potted versions. Even Lawton, in a useful attempt to produce a simplified account of this work, confesses that there are parts which were not comprehensible to him.[15]

Particular attention is necessary for words linking figures. The distortion here has come to be called the 'fully-only' technique.[16] Differences are described as 'fully' X per cent when the objective is to show a relationship, but 'only' X per cent when the aim is to suggest that no relationship exists. There are many common variations on this ploy. 'Twenty of the samples were selected for detailed study' usually means that the others did not look promising if the results were to confirm the hypothesis and were ignored. 'Typical result are shown' probably means that the best were picked out. 'Correct within an order of magnitude' may mean it was more wrong than right.

Another popular technique could be called stage army mobilisation. Here it is implied that the results presented are backed by all the other researchers who matter. 'It has been long known that' may mean it has just been thought out. 'It is generally believed that' may mean that a few others have speculated along the same line. 'The results are in line with major studies in this field' means that the point has been a matter of dispute. In some cases the mobilisation is predicted. 'The need now is for further research', 'Much additional work will now be required for full understanding' and 'the research will continue as resources become available,' all mean that the author does not understand the results, but is looking for a new grant to carry on trying.

Finally the written account can be wrapped up in the conventional language of science labelled by Watkins as didactic dead-pan.[17] Scientists report their work in an impersonal, stylised manner that suppresses personal opinion and experience. Technical language is used to give the impression of absolutely reliable methods, unaffected by the personality and social life of the scientist involved. Scientists stage-manage the impression they give to their public.

References for prestige

The legitimate use of references is to alert the reader to the existence of relevant work that illustrates and supports the point put forward by the author. It acts as a shorthand to those who share a discipline, summing up whole areas of evidence with a single name. First the references are selected to support a viewpoint and secondly they can become ends in themselves. An absence of references is suspicious, but so is a surfeit. The first possible misuse of references to look out for is over-abundance. When every line is littered with (Smith 1960) or (Brown 1961) the suspicion is that the author is boosting his case. The second misuse is the mobilisation of famous names to place the work on a par with the established. Dedicating the book to Hans, Talcott or Basil, writing it in memory of Bertrand, acknowledging a debt to Noam can serve the same function as a Soviet tribute to Stalin as the greatest scientist and Lysenko as his greatest discipline.

Such a muster of names also protects the author from criticism. Anyone on first name terms with the great and who acknowledges how much he owes to the advanced seminar at Harvard is unlikely to be the target of critical hatchet men. Furthermore, filling the work with references to the established increases the chance of getting it published as the referees used by journals and publishing firms will see no harm in further publicising their work. In a small specialism within a subject publishing its own journal, a few on the inside refer to each other while those trying to get in have to distribute their references diplomatically to get their work accepted. Oldcom found a correlation of 0.96 between footnote references to the chairman of the doctoral committee and the successful completion of 100 Ph.D. dissertations.[18] The reference is a neat way of combining flattery with erudition.

The second ploy is the use of the obscure and exotic. No one is likely to look up references to the *Revista Iberoamericana de Seguridad Social* and there are abstracting services which enable the author to find unlikely examples. Better still are references to unpublished Ph.D. theses in obscure foreign universities who are loath to let anything leave their archives. Another variation to look for is a concentration on long foreign-sounding names. Smith and Brown sound like amateurs compared with Raskolnikov and Skavar. The Vienna School is more impressive than the Department in Birmingham.

The third target should be the ingratiating truism. 'As Kilroy has conclusively shown, orphans have no parents', is a model of many attempts to flatter. A fourth ploy to detect is the professional trump. Here the reference indicates to the reader that he does not share the company that the author keeps and therefore cannot challenge the written account. 'Participants at the recent congress in Bokhara will confirm,' neatly places the reader outside the jet-set Pale. Another variation is to refer to verbal communications or correspondence, preferably with some august academic. For the reader the healthy response is to ask what is being concealed by this deviousness, rather than any acceptance that truth has been revealed through contact with an oracle.

Extreme window-dressing in the form reported here is uncommon. However, the difference between lay and professional audiences produces a dilemma for all researchers and writers. An easy, simple style of reporting may reach a large audience, but not convey the complexity of the methods or results. Giving full technical details may restrict the audience to a small, sophisticated circle.

This dilemma can be seen in Cane and Schroeder's study *The Teacher and Research*.[19] Here teachers' opinions on educational research were collected. Three-quarters of the teachers never saw the *British Journal of Educational Psychology* or *Educational Research*. They were opposed to the use of technical jargon, statistical tables and theorising. They even felt that Schools Council publications, written specially for teachers, were too complicated. Yet while demanding simplicity, these teachers were aware that potted, simplified reports left out the detail that was necessary for assessment of reliability and validity.

This report by Cane and Schroeder confirms the need for a more widespread knowledge of the status of evidence derived from research. The teachers suspected that values were mixed up with the research. They guessed that samples were often inadequate and unrepresentative. They detected that extraneous variables could have often accounted for results. They were suspicious of generalisations. What was missing was any systematic knowledge of the process of assessment. Without it the tendency was to reject all research rather than sorting out the good from the poor.

HOW PREJUDICED ARE THE BRITISH?

Investigating the relations between racial groups in Britain has rightly been a major occupation of social scientists. But as Moore has argued, the concentration on a social problem and the publication of evidence for purely pragmatic reasons, nevertheless involves putting forward a particular view of society.[1] Most of the researchers have assumed the desirability of social homogeneity, value-consensus and freedom from conflict. They have designed their surveys to measure the extent to which these ideals are being realised. In doing so they have tended to ignore the historical, comparative and sociological context of race relations. As a consequence, the interpretation of the descriptive evidence has been as varied and conflicting as the political views of those involved in the debate.

There are two difficulties in interpreting descriptive studies. First, there is no baseline from which comparisons can be made. There is no standard for an unprejudiced population, or the prejudice to be expected in a class-ridden or classless society. Any figure of the proportions which seem prejudiced can be interpreted as satisfactory or outrageous according to the values held by the interpreter. Second, the questions asked may have no relation to the social structure within which race relations are determined. It may be that beliefs about race are only reflections of class consciousness. It may be that discrimination against minorities is only part of a social structure based on the domination of one class by another. It may be that race relations can be seen only as an index of the extent to which minorities are integrated into a society of plural value systems and fluid groups. But surveys without theoretical reference cannot give an answer.

In the late summer of 1958 the first race riots on any scale took place in Nottingham and Notting Hill. This not only brought the worries over increased immigration into the open, but raised the question whether the British were prejudiced against coloured people. In the ten years that followed there were seven major attempts to measure attitudes on racial issues, culminating in the study conducted in 1968 by Research Services Limited for the Institute of Race Relations as part of its study on *Colour and Citizenship*.[2] The report of this study, running to 800 pages, has been described as a 'royal commission', set up by the Institute of Race Relations and financed by the Nuffield Foundation.

At a conference on Race Relations of the British Sociological Association held shortly before publication, the need for the evidence the report would contain became clear for none available was adequate. It was favourably reviewed after publication, but only when it was referred to as policy-oriented research at its best[3] did critics attack those parts of it relating to the attitudes of the public and which were based on a social survey. The result of the ensuing debate over the status of the evidence leaves the problem of the level of racial prejudice in Britain as open as ever.[4]

The survey for the Institute of Race Relations was recommended by a group of social scientists acting as advisers to the Study of Race Relations. The field work was done between December 1966 and April 1967. The sample consisted of 2,500 white adults divided equally between Lambeth, Ealing, Wolverhampton, Nottingham and Bradford. Another 2,250 whites were interviewed as a control group, using a more limited range of questions than those used with the experimental group. The questions were designed to place those interviewed along a scale of attitudes ranging from highly prejudiced to tolerant, through intermediate points of prejudice-inclined and tolerant-inclined.

The major criticisms were directed at this scale for measuring tolerance.[5] First the book mentions four key and ten supplementary questions that formed this scale, but only contains the four crucial ones. Second, critics maintained that four items could only produce a crude scale. Third, the scale was criticised as containing three out of four questions concerned with housing and with having a built-in bias towards tolerance. Fourth, the scale was criticised as incapable of discriminating between the majority who fell between extreme tolerance and prejudice. The authors were indeed very cautious about treating the three-quarters who were prejudice-inclined or tolerant-inclined as distinct groups. Fifth, the questions were criticised as too long, one of the four consisting of twenty-seven words. Sixth, there seemed to have been no testing of the reliability or validity of the scale.

The reply made by Abrams of Research Services Limited, who contributed the criticised chapter, was that the compression of the original chapter from 20,000 to 14,000 words accounted for the lack of information from which the reliability of the evidence could be assessed and for the omission of the complete questionnaire.[6] The power of the scale to discriminate and the presentation of the results were defended as suitable for a book designed for the general reader.

Finally, the critics, in replies to Abram's defence of the survey, reaffirmed their criticism and commented on the inadequacy of his defence.[7] The point was made that if the scale was constructed as Abrams maintained, the book was misleading and contained contradictory statements about its construction. The second point was made that the survey was terribly misleading in lumping as tolerant many people of different degrees of prejudice, including some who may have been very prejudiced but who could not have been detected by this scale.

This debate ranged over only one of the thirty-three chapters in the book. Yet this chapter is crucial as it is the one that depends on a specially designed survey. The results are used to make comparisons with other survey results and to outline the attitudes of the British public on a range of key issues concerning the housing, employment and mobility of immigrants and their relation with white adults. The book was to provide a basis for informed policy decisions. Yet the one part that was concerned with apparently hard facts was challenged as having a soft centre.

It was in the interpretation of these results that the real dispute occurred. Regardless of the technical standing of the research, publication was a signal for acrimony. There were those who saw the evidence as a sign of improving relations and of the fundamental decency of the British. Others saw the findings as yet another symptom of a class society dominated by capitalist values and the politics of coercion. Others dismissed them as irrelevant and a further sign of the impotence of social scientists to effect social change and do anything but help shore up a decaying system by providing convenient statistics.

The difficulty in assessing the relations between races in Britain can also be gauged from the debate between Rex and Moore in their study in Birmingham[8] and Davies and Taylor in Newcastle upon Tyne.[9] Rex and Moore in their book, *Race, Community and Conflict*, saw discrimination as forcing immigrants into neighbourhoods and into particular types of housing. Davies and Taylor in their article, 'Race, community and no conflict', found that immigrants were not forced into accepting certain types of housing but actually preferred it and chose it. This controversy in letters to *New Society*[10] includes not only claims that evidence refutes the views of the other pair of authors but challenges to the reliability of the other study. The conclusion that can be drawn from this correspondence is a recurring one. Each pair of authors seems to have sprung from their different ideological viewpoints. Those who feel that the world is basically harmonious take comfort from evidence that simultaneously confirms the coercive nature of human relations for those holding a view of the world as a cockpit.

11

THE INTERPRETATION OF RESULTS

Ideally the processing and interpretation of data collected through research should be determined as the whole work is planned. But this is rarely possible in the social sciences. Research takes time and as circumstances change, so do the questions that need an answer. Even if there is a precise hypothesis to guide the work, there will be unexpected aspects among the data collected. In most research the observations and questions are left open-ended to allow for the unpredictable. Social researchers are alert to the unexpected, the serendipitous, for this is liable to be the most exciting. Data collected on human behaviour is never mundane and researchers live in anticipation of the novel. This open-ended perception of research also allows the social researcher freedom in interpreting data.

Modern techniques of data processing allow complex analyses to be made. Where the researchers of the 1940s and earlier worked out their own statistics or pushed their own knitting needles through Cope-Chat cards, their successors program computers. This has several side-effects. For example, it ensures that the data is in a readily retrievable form. Burt and his contemporaries would have worked out their results by hand, on the backs of envelopes. Even Cope-Chat cards were soon thrown away. Today the results remain on computer tape or disc. But the computer, and even the desk calculator, also enables the researcher to program for multi-variate analyses that would have been beyond the dreams of researchers even twenty years ago. The researcher can look over the computer printout and be very selective over the results to publish. He can run cross-tabulations until something interesting turns up. This is a cause for caution when looking at statistical presentations of survey and experimental results. As researchers interpret their data thay can become artists with sophisticated technology.

Irrefutable interpretations

To Popper, the essence of scientific ectivity is the scrutiny of evidence to uncover flaws.[1] Science is based on the confirmation or rejection of hypotheses. But this means that the hypotheses have to be falsifiable. In a similar way, the interpretations of data can be stated in forms that are refutable by reference to established knowledge. Other researchers can replicate the study to see if the results still stand, and readers can assess the chances that the results were false. But it is also possible to state results so that they are not open to this critical replication or scrutiny. Such interpretations have the additional danger that they look even more convincing because they can not be refuted. Yet the social sciences, as well as the natural sciences, are littered with such forgotten debris. Mainly because the research concerned was unrelated to any established tradition, because the concepts used were not defined by reference to any established tradition, because they were not defined by reference to any established theory, and because the terms used in interpretation had no framework for definition, they were of transitory interest only. This applies in particular to the study of education where many social sciences are employed, but where the research has no unified frame of reference. Educational 'facts' frequently have no grounding beyond the specific research. Their credibility is dubious.

Between 1920 and 1960 there were eighty-three studies of teacher effectiveness carried out in the School of Education, University of Wisconsin. These produced 183 measures of teacher effectiveness. But in a monograph written within this department summing up this effort, none were seen as satisfactory and every new investigation had used a fresh one.[2] Little that was reliable or useable had been produced. This teacher effectiveness industry was not confined to Wisconsin. Much of the work is completely convincing within its own terms of reference. But there is no reference beyond that, and unique definition ensures that comparisons with other work are impossible. Because refutation was impossible, the poor had to be accepted with the good. There was no accumulation of evidence. Everyone started at the beginning.

It can be argued that the ability to isolate the features of an effective teacher is so important that research is essential. The same would apply to many other important subjects on which evidence has been presented in older books on educational psychology or sociology. There is plenty of evidence on the effectiveness of programmed learning, discovery methods, learning by objectives, and no doubt of earlier innovations now largely forgotten such as the Dalton Plan and the Play Way. There are numerous theories of intelligence and personality backed by empirical studies. The history of child development studies is littered with macabre interpretations of the behaviour of young children and of the efficacy of treatments. The psychologists concerned were not sadists or lunatics. They were merely optimists about their own work and its independent merit. They forgot that scepticism is a response based firmly on the coffins of the previously irrefutable.

Impractical interpretations

There is always a tension between policy-makers expecting concrete suggestions for action from social research, and researchers, trying to present a simple picture of a complicated scene. The evaluations of intervention programmes such as the Educational Priority Area schemes, or the Community Development Projects inevitably produce reports that rightly maintain that the spending of a few thousand pounds is unlikely to counter the effects of centuries of urban decay, or the lack of impact among existing social services. But in such cases the interpretation, although not what the policy makers wanted, is practical. If the politicians insist on cosmetic programmes and ask for evaluations, they will get non-significant results and interpretations that explain why no significant results should be expected.

However, there are times when the researcher, interested in affecting practical affairs rather than improving a theoretical model, selects factors for investigation that have little relevance for action. It may for example be interesting that Catholic primary schools have higher reading scores than others, but conversion to Catholicism is not within the powers of the Local Education Authority. It may be true that the only way to raise educational attainment in inner city schools is to produce a balanced social class mix in the catchment areas. But this isn't much use to the hard-pressed educational administrator, and would necessitate draconian social engineering.

Problems of selection arise in the selection of variables for study. If the object of research is to examine the causes of crime, the factors chosen are likely to be structural, concerned with the social and economic backgrounds of the groups under investigation. But if the object is to recommend ways of reducing crime, the focus has to be on factors which are changeable. The capitalist class structure may be the root cause, but if action is needed it might be more immediately helpful to look at ways of increasing the oversight of juveniles by adults or the way the police process cases. One of the reasons why the publication of *Fifteen Thousand Hours* by Rutter *et al.* in 1978 was welcomed was that it contained evidence that could be used to raise performance within schools.[3] Studies where the focus was on individual children very often produced results related to social backgrounds or psychological traits, where it was difficult to see what action could follow.

Selective interpretations

The most common bias in interpreting evidence comes from the selection for discussion of only such of the data as fits the hypothesis. This is difficult to detect, as written accounts rarely contain enough information to reveal such selectivity. A thesis contains the full account. A book based on it contains only that deemed saleable by the publisher. A 'reader' or summary removes what is left. What is removed is usually the technical section on methods. This is why 'readers', digests and symposia are dangerous and why original sources are best. The latter contain the detail needed for full assessment, the former contain only the juicy but boned parts.

An example of progressive simplification can be found in the very influential and well-designed study of different styles of leadership by Lewin, Lippitt and White.[4] In most summaries of this work the superiority of the democratic style seems unquestionable. The original accounts by the author are more cautious. But only in the fuller of these original accounts are there results that throw doubt on the performance of groups under democratic leaders. For example, some of the evidence suggests that if productivity is a priority, authoritarian leadership may be superior.[5] Again, in fuller accounts there are details of the results when groups were criticised by a hostile stranger. Democratic and *laissez-faire* groups seemed to be prone to vent their feelings on other groups. It could be argued that 'wars' occur in frustrated democracies and that the best hope for peace among men lies in authoritarian regimes.[6]

Frequently the arguments between authors and reviewers or other critics revolve round this selectivity. The critics maintain that the evidence presented does not convince or that an alternative or conflicting explanation is possible. The author often replies that shortage of space meant that crucial evidence had to be left out. The criticism that the methods used and the evidence presented do not justify the conclusions made by the authors has occurred many times in this book. Piaget's studies of child development, the Authoritarian Personality research, *Colour and Citizenship*, Coleman's analysis of adolescent society, the follow-up of children by Douglas, the *Polish Peasant* by Thomas and Znaniecki and the historical work of Leach, Simon and Jordan have all been subjected to this criticism. Yet these were chosen because they were among the most influential and the most respected studies in education, history and the social sciences.

Fallacious interpretations

In many of the controversies reported in this book evidence appears contradictory. Large-scale surveys suggest that the larger the size of school classes, the higher the attainment. But small-scale studies suggest the opposite. Even more alarming and fundamental, large-scale statistical studies such as the Coleman Report on *Equality of Educational Opportunity*,[7] and Jencks on *Inequality: A Reassessment of the Effect of Family and Schooling in America*[8] concluded that attainment seems unrelated to the school attended. Yet smaller scale studies such as Rutter, Maughan,

Mortimore and Ouston's study of twelve secondary schools[9] and similar scale studies by Reynolds,[10] Power[11] and Gath[12] have shown that schools do make a difference, not only to attainment, but to delinquency, attendance and behaviour generally.

Part of the contradiction is explained by the very narrow range of attainments that were measured in the large-scale studies. As the attainment taken into account relates closer to school subject, even large-scale studies begin to show school effects. Schools may not be able to compensate for society, but they are not impotent. With small-scale comparisons, schools with intakes from similar social backgrounds produced very different results. But the results were not on aspects of behaviour that could be easily measured in large-scale studies.

But the most important reason for the apparent contradiction probably lies in the level of analysis. Critics of Bennett's *Teaching Styles and Pupil Progress* argued that if the school class rather than the individual children had been taken as the unit of analysis results may have been very different.[13] Similarly, Coleman relied on the verbal ability scores of his 645,000 pupils, distributed among 4,000 schools.[14] But to interpret overall school performance from the aggregated scores of children on a single test is to ignore features of schools that are more than the sum of those pupil scores. Similarly, it may be misleading to draw conclusions about individuals from measures of collective behaviour such as crime, birth or migration rates. Criminal statistics are a poor base for statements about individual motivation to commit crime, just as a knowledge of the motives of individual suicides is an inadequate source of information about the morale of a nation.

Alker details eight fallacies that are possible in analysis.[15] Riley has added two more where, although the actual research fits the theoretical model, the analysis sticks so close to a single level that information necessary for full understanding is concealed.[16] Psychologistic fallacies occur where a researcher ignores facts about social groupings in explanation. Sociologistic fallacies occur where information on individuals is ignored. Thus psychologists have tended to ignore the uniformity and predictability of suicide rates while concentrating on individuals' states of mind, while sociologists have been contented to generalise from suicide rates and ignore the insights from studies of those who tried and failed.

A similar shift in level of analysis often occurs in the study of organisations and the roles of individuals within them.[17] Sociologists are concerned with the structure, but to explain the effect on the individuals concerned fall back on psychological concepts such as internalisation and alienation. Thus role is used by the sociologist as behaviour which individuals occupying a particular position feel constrained to follow. But to explain why individuals actually behave in a predictable, regular way there is a switch to explanation in terms of the effect of the role on behaviour. The focus is on the organisation and data is collected with this in mind. But the individual is linked to this organisation by assumptions about individual personality and behaviour. The consequence has often been a picture of men in organisations as passively responding to pressures rather than active and often disruptive participants.

Disembodied interpretations

A common tendency is to produce evidence, but bye-pass it while interpreting. This is a common danger given the real nature of scientific endeavour. The researcher starts with a hunch and ends with a certainty. The evidence presented in between may, however, not prove an adequate link between them. This seems to have happened in Musgrove and Taylor's study, *Society and the Teacher's Role*.[18] Conclusions about the despotic nature of teachers, the exclusion of parental interests from schools and the need to cultivate, not eliminate, charisma in teachers under training appear in a concluding chapter. Yet there is little apparent relation between these conclusions and the very useful evidence presented in the previous six chapters of the book.[19]

Similarly the immense labours of Jordan to trace the philanthropic efforts of English merchants and professional men after the Reformation have left a mass of valuable evidence.[20] But Jordan's conclusions about the extent and nature of this charity rest less on this evidence than on his assumptions. Despite the amount of evidence collected it is still confined mainly to the merchant and professional classes and largely ignores other forms of charity by other groups. Yet Jordan's conclusions refer to the whole English scene, though there is no adequate basis for such a generalisation.

A final example is Riesman's *The Lonely Crowd*,[21] a best seller in social science, half a million copies having been sold of the paperback version published in 1954. Larrabee saw this popularity as a symptom of an urge to national self-analysis in the USA at this time.[22] The personality types suggested as paramount in different historical periods have become part of the language of sociology. But there is doubt over the interpretation of contemporary life that was presented. Riesman and Glazer, looking back after eleven years, admitted that they had serious misgivings about their thesis even before publication but decided to go ahead.[23] They admitted overestimating the degree of social change and the links between character and society. They also admitted that their analysis was incomplete, leaving out particularly such factors as the distribution of power which they later saw was crucial in understanding contemporary America.

Deceptive interpretations

A third and more serious but less common fault is to wrap up a slanted study in an academic package. Some idea of the ease with which research can be used to support a cause can be gained from the article published in 1961 by Wiggins and Schoeck, 'A profile of ageing: U.S.A.'[24] This appeared in the journal *Geriatrics* devoted to diseases and processes of ageing. In appearance it is a conventional, provisional report of a survey organised by two professors of sociology. The methods described are convincing. A sample of 1,492 old persons were probability-sampled from seventy-eight areas, stratified by sex, socio-economic level, residence and geographical division. The authors admit that non-whites were under-represented because of shortage of funds, but claim that each old person in the area sampled had an equal chance of being selected. A table shows that the sample was close in age distribution, marital status and religious reference to the national figure in the US census.

Here is an apparently systematic survey. Yet the research had already become notorious after one of the authors had read a paper based on it to a conference of gerontologists in San Francisco a year before.[25] This notoriety and the scrutiny of the methods used to collect the data were the consequence of presenting results contradicting all the available evidence and the policy of the profession. The critics had the full support of their colleagues to investigate and criticise. In reality the research turned out to be highly suspect. The sampling had been loaded to produce a profile of the aged as generally in good health, energetically independent and secure within family and community bonds. Yet only through the furore caused by the original paper did the overloading of the sample with more wealthy old persons come to light.

There is irony in the publication in 1960 of a collection of articles by Wiggins and Schoeck under the title *Scientism and Values*.[26] This attacks the tendency in the social sciences to concentrate on building pseudoscientific models and on producing quantitative data at the expense of insight into real problems. Thus at the time when authors were gathering together articles to expose the pretensions of local scientists, they were engaged in research that was designed so as to support the stand of the American Medical Association against free medical care for the aged.

HOW FORMATIVE IS INFANTILE EXPERIENCE?

Many of the controversies in this book are of academic interest only. But some have important practical implications. The most remarkable example of an academic theory that led to profound and rapid changes in social policy was the notion that experiences in the first few years of life left an indelible impression on adult personality. In particular, the Maternal Deprivation Theory was used as a justification for changing hospital routines for young children, had an immediate impact on attitudes and practices in caring for children, and was used to accelerate the closure of large children's homes. Above all the theory that adult personality was determined very early in life and that recovery from early deprivation caused by separation from the mother was unlikely, was used to bring pressure to bear on mothers to stay with their children and not leave them for work, holiday or sickness.

The evidence backing this theory was used dogmatically. Linked to psychoanalytic theory, which was the base for many deterministic hypotheses, the work of Bowlby and others suggested that permanent damage resulted from the separation of mother and child when the latter was young.[1] Goldfarb for example concluded that lasting harm was done if there was a separation in the first two years of life and that there was no recovery.[2] Bowlby even maintained that those who opposed the idea that mothers should devote themselves entirely to their children were themselves manifesting their own suffering from maternal deprivation.[3] Spock maintained that the deprived child would turn out to be incapable of loving anyone.[4] *Maternal Care and Mental Health* was published by the World Health Organisation in 1951. The popular version was published by Penguin Books in 1953 as *Child Care and the Growth of Love*.[5] These books were based not only on Bowlby's own research, but on that of Goldfarb, and also on the work of Spitz,[6] showing the disastrous impact of institutional care on infants. This evidence was used as a basis for a rapid reorganisation of child care services and for a drastic revision in attitudes towards the role of mothers of young children.

By the late 1950s psychologists were already questioning the value of the concept of maternal deprivation. In 1959, Wootton, in the blunt, sceptical style that has made her such a valuable antidote to sloppy thinking in the social sciences, pointed out the loose definitions that made the evidence an unreliable basis for determining the extent, incidence and causes of disturbance through deprivation.[7] Evidence was soon produced showing that recovery from early deprivation did occur. In 1972, Rutter in an assessment of available evidence concluded that there was no firm basis to support the theory.[8] In 1975, Morgan published a swingeing attack on the psychological foundations of the theory, the original research on which it was based and the naive way in which it was translated into policy.[9] In 1976, Clarke and Clarke gathered together evidence to show that the importance of the early years in determining adult personality had been grossly exaggerated and that the resilience of children had been underestimated.[10] The effects of maternal deprivation were rarely immutable. The time taken for the evidence on maternal deprivation to be established, acted upon and then demolished was short. Bowlby's evidence appeared in 1952. O'Connor published the first criticism of the evidence in 1956.[11] Within twenty years there had been a reversal to seeing the early years as important, but not indelible in effect.

It is however necessary to avoid dogmatism in attacking maternal deprivation and other theories. Just as there is a danger that evidence will be stretched too far to support a theory, so there is a danger that the pendulum will be pushed back too far when the critiques are mounted. There is little doubt that the early years are important.[12] There is also little doubt that if an infant remains long in a situation where attachment to a caring adult is denied, the chances of growing up capable of forming caring relations are slight. The maternal deprivation theory was pushed too far. But not enough is known to be dogmatic about the resilience of children. Early experiences may have long-lasting effects and to jettison this with Bowlby's theory would be irresponsible. Human life is complicated, and explanations of human behaviour are consequently unlikely to be simple. If evidence turns out to be fallible it is usually because the researcher has been unable to take all the important factors into account, or to appreciate their importance or existence. For example, it may be that the evidence on the admission to hospital of young children suggests that there is only a temporary effect on behaviour. But both Douglas,[13] and Quinton and Rutter,[14] found a link between repeated admissions to hospital and disturbance in behaviour in later childhood. Similarly, intervention programmes to raise the attainment of young children may seem to have only temporary impact, but longer-term follow-up studies suggest that there may be gains that appear later.

Above all, it is safest to be sceptical when researchers write with certainty. This is particularly important where past events in infancy are supposed to determine present behaviour. The conclusion can easily be drawn that nothing can be done to help a disturbed or backward junior or adolescent. The focus is on some buried event. The organisation of care or education, or health need not be considered. Those who justify lack of effort to raise attainment in the present by reference to past events receive too much support from evidence that justifies their fatalism.

It is significant that Rutter, whose 'Maternal Deprivation Reassessed' was published in 1972, had already started work studying the children who were followed into the secondary schools that formed the sample for his *Fifteen Thousand Hours* published in 1979.[15] That book suggests that secondary schools do affect the children that attend them. Academic attainment, behaviour, delinquency and job obtained after leaving all seem related to the school attended. This conclusion is optimistic. It means that teachers can benefit children through the way they organise their schools, despite the social background from which the children come or their early experiences. This research suggests that early deprivation could not result in immutable defects. If maternal deprivation or early determination of intelligence, or personality were not remediable, schools in some deprived areas might as well be holiday camps with maximum possible security.

12

THE SCOPE AND LIMITATIONS OF SOCIAL RESEARCH

Social researchers may never win. If they confirm the folklore their work is criticised as a waste of time. If they refute that folklore they aren't believed. But research does transform the unrecognised into the obvious. It is now folklore that there are extensive social class differences in educational attainment. Anyone researching to confirm this today would be accused of wasting public funds. Yet twenty-five years ago the evidence was startling. When Barker Lunn produced the first evidence on streaming from a large scale-study in 1970 and showed that there was no dramatic difference in attainment resulting from different methods in grouping and schools, neither the supporters of streaming nor their opponents would believe her.[1] Today the comparison is not worth making in the same terms. When Power and Morris reported in 1967 that similar schools produced different rates of delinquency among their pupils, the local teachers were so incensed that the research had to stop.[2] In 1978 Rutter's work came to the same conclusion and there were no protests.[3]

Research is only one influence on current beliefs and practices, but it carries prestige and can often produce the only systematically collected evidence. There are serious limitations on social research, but the scope remains broad. Each researcher is a pioneer, for the research can never be an exact technical replication of any previous work, and the social world is never the same twice. Policy-makers are hungry for information and researchers are in the information game, whether fact-grubbing or theory-launching. There are always more problems than researchers to examine them. In this chapter the contribution of social research to making policy, from the humble to the ambitious, will be examined, first through the contribution that can be made, and second, through the way the evidence is used.

The contribution of social research

It was argued in Chapter 2 that theory and research could not be separated, as each depends upon the existence of the other. Research can be ranged from the descriptive at one extreme and the theoretical at the other, but this can be misleading. All research is pervaded with theory. But descriptive research is also liable to affect theory building. Theories are also of interest to policy-makers. But whereas academics look to research to improve the theoretical model, policy-makers look to it to see if the theory has been confirmed to an extent that gives confidence in it as a basis for action.[4] Thus distinctions between policy-orientated and conclusion-orientated, pure and applied, research are largely meaningless. It is impossible to classify research in advance into that which will be of use to practitioners and that of use to academics.

Let us take two extreme cases and one intermediate, where evidence has been directly influential. First is the production of one simple statistic within a report on the 1973 stage of the Inner London Education Authority's *Literacy Survey*.[5] At this stage the children studied were in their third year of secondary school. The bulk of the evidence produced was on reading standards at this stage, and between this and previous stages. But the form of organisation of English teaching in the junior forms of the secondary schools had been collected and the proportion of schools in which English was taught in mixed ability groups was included in the evidence. This statistic turned out to be a bombshell. The extent of mixed ability grouping had not been appreciated. The authority rapidly organised an inspectorate enquiry and in-service courses. It is not always the large-scale research that turns out to be important.

Another illustration of this unanticipated nature of evidence is Hargreaves's *Social Relations in a Secondary School*.[6] This book is a study of one secondary modern school in the early 1960s. It is still quoted as evidence on the perils of streaming in the 1980s. Social researchers never know when their work, however humble, is going to be influential, and they carry a heavy responsibility as a consequence. That is why there has been such an emphasis in this book on the need to give readers the chance of judging credibility.

Hargreaves's book was theoretically insightful and carefully researched. It is a good example of the possibilities of one-man research in the social sciences, where everyone works at the frontiers. At the more academic end of the spectrum of influential research is labelling theory developed within criminology and embraced enthusiastically and romantically within education. This passion has been met among teachers, lecturers, inspectors, advisers and above all among politicians. The idea that a frown, a poor mark or relegation can stigmatise a child and hence produce the low attainment is attractive. It enables those outside the schools to blame the attitude of teachers for failures among the children. But it also enables teachers to justify the removal of the measures of low attainment as these are part of the labelling process. Hence the basis of the criticism is removed. The hatchet work on the often-quoted Rosenthal and Jacobson *Pygmalion in the Classroom* study,[7] Nash's evidence that children are capable of grading each other,[8] and the failure of the message itself to raise attainment, have not been discouraging. It should have been easy for teachers to go around smiling, treating all children as bright equals and hence keep them all motivated and achieving. That labelling may be context-bound, restricted and over-simplified as suggested by the available evidence, has not weakened much of the ardour.

These three illustrations of the impact of social research suggest that the oft-found pessimism of social researchers over their influence on events is misplaced. The problem is not that research is ignored, but that it is accepted too readily and too selectively. This book was written in the hope that it would provide some guide to the selection of the reliable and valid. During its revision, after six years in local government, this guidance seems even more imperative. That experience outside academia has also shown the need for researchers to be scrupulous in presenting their work so that the reader can give it due weight. It also showed the need for researchers to accept responsibility for disseminating their work to those who might use it. If researchers have complained of lack of impact, or misinterpretation, it is their own fault. They produce evidence that is often all that is available for policy-makers who are on the lookout for it. But the researcher's interest often wanes just as the evidence is available for the public. The next stage or the next project is more attractive than public relations work on the old.

Direct influences on policy are probably less common than the steady alteration of opinions about human behaviour and interaction as the social and behavioural sciences are reported in the media, at conferences and through pre- and in-service education. Explanations of human behaviour are continually changing. Psychological views of child development are typical. The professional opinions of fifty years ago now seems macabre. Even the stress on critical stages of development that dominated teacher education in the 1960s are replaced in the 1970s by a model of a single and continuous critical period.[9] The practical effects of this change have still to work their way into child-rearing and education, for the views of the 1960s still dominate teacher education in the early 1980s.

As the professionals produce new evidence and alter their own views of human development, changes occur in the relevant social institutions. It is impossible to detect any precise relation. It may be that the relation is two-way, or that there are third factors at work. For example, Getzels has traced four stages of elementary school design in the United States and four apparently closely related conceptions of the way children learn.[10] Early in this century children were seen as empty organisms to be filled with knowledge by teachers. Their desks were ranked so they focused on the teacher. When the learner was seen as active in learning through a far-from-empty personality, the classroom was altered to move the teacher to an inconspicuous position. Then, with a stress on the importance of interpersonal relations, classrooms were designed to allow movement and for groups to form. But all these theories of learning, persisting into the 1950s, assumed drives, and reduction of needs as the motives for learning. From the 1950s, children were seen not to be reducing a need, but to be active seekers of knowledge for its own sake. The open classroom allowed this exploration to happen.

Getzels denies that he is suggesting that this is necessarily progress. Nor is he suggesting that there is any established cause and effect. He also acknowledges that other influences on design were present. But he is suggesting that research, especially academic research, which helps alter conceptions of human behaviour, rather than feeding directly into policy, has a profound impact on the context in which policy is made. As examples he picks the work of Lewin, Lippitt and White,[11] and of Piaget,[12] along with that of Thorndike and Woodworth[13] that undermined the idea of transfer of training, the justification of mind-building exercises and for the teaching of Latin and Greek. It is worrying however that the psychological theories have changed so fast and so dramatically. Anxiety is increased even further by the lag in the introduction of new conceptions into the preparation of teachers. If Getzels's account is correct, the different classrooms of the 1930s, 1950s and 1970s would contain teachers whose pedagogy would be based on theories belonging to a previous design and outdated conceptions of learning.

The test of natural science is the ability to predict or project. While these are not the criteria that many social scientists would now accept for judging the utility of their work, they remain important for the policy-maker. From the teacher in the classrooom wondering whether he can act confidently on the evidence on the relation of teaching styles to pupil practice, to the politician looking at the evidence on the relation of class sizes to pupil attainment as he decides on the allocation of resources, the predictive reliability of evidence is central. Furthermore, some evidence is produced specifically to aid planning. Demography is an example where the projection of future populations is a basic factor in determining most government policy. Yet this is a minefield.

In 1938, Charles predicted that the population of Great Britain in the year 2000 would be between 18 and 32 million.[14] Projections by the Central Statistical Office for the turn of the century follow.

In 1955 the population for the year 2000 was projected as 50 million
In 1960 the population for the year 2000 was projected as 62 million
In 1965 the population for the year 2000 was projected as 73 million
In 1970 the population for the year 2000 was projected as 63 million
In 1974 the population for the year 2000 was projected as 58 million.[15]

These figures are projections not predictions. The demographers are tracing existing trends forward. But the consequences for policy of such fluctuations have been serious. Across the last forty years there have been dire warnings about declining population and near panics about over-population. Charles estimated a population in 2035 of only 5 million.[16] Projections in the early 1960s for that year would have been around 100 million.

The difficulty in forecasting population lies behind some of the blunders over social policy. Housing need was under-estimated after the sophisticated 1951 Census because births were about to rise. The same period saw the approval of the three-year training college course for teachers. This was planned to give no output from the colleges in 1963, when it was predicted that the post-war bulge would have passed through the schools, thus reducing the demand for teachers. In reality the infant schools were bulging with children born in the mid-1950s. The rise and fall in births has proved to be a continuing source of problems. We now have a surplus of teachers. The figures produced in the Robbins Committee report on demand for higher education were outdated within five years.[17] The 1957 Willink Committee forecast a falling demand for doctors, recommended a reduced intake of medical students and only succeeded in strengthening the bargaining position of doctors, leaving the Health Service under-manned.[18] In practice these difficulties were exacerbated by belief in the economic dogma that demand determines supply. That supply determines demand in social services was only accepted by the relevant government minister in 1969.[19]

However, demographers aren't to blame for not predicting changes in the number of births, or for failing to anticipate migrations whether voluntary, or enforced by an Amin, a famine or the reluctance to stay under communist or fascist regimes. When demographers can project over a short time span they can be very accurate. The fall in births that started in 1965 and persisted for over a decade has produced a number of projections of future numbers. In the 1970s techniques have been improved and high, low and central variants drawn. The policy-maker is now given a number of possibilities and planning can be contingent on any of these. The fall in school rolls consequent on the fall in births after the mid-1960s has produced a dramatic cut in the numbers of teachers being trained. Colleges, expanded in the 1960s to meet rising demand, were cut as projected numbers fell in the 1970s. This has been a success story for demographers even if the policy-makers have been culpable. The projection of numbers in school over a period of ten or even twenty years is liable to be accurate. Once the births for a year are known it is easy to project forward to the key years of five, eleven and eighteen. Even on the local scene, where migration is a complicating factor, the percentage loss or gain in any year group can be calculated and used for projection. What is striking about the contraction and projected contraction of education is how reluctant those involved were to accept the figures. This is another indication that researchers can not win. When population projections are demanded so far ahead that it has to become guesswork, demographers are blamed for mistakes. When the time-span is short enough for them to be accurate they are not believed. The pianist is often shot because the tune is disliked.

Thus the researcher who serves policy-makers is under pressure. If the usual response to his work is that he has wasted time and money, he is at risk when the evidence produced is dramatic. The long history of attempts at intervening in social and educational conditions to affect positive discrimination has produced many examples of this dilemma. The evaluations of the various projects in education have generally shown little impact, although later studies suggest that there may be longer-term gains.[20] Similarly the succession of projects to improve community life have been shown to be disappointing in their impact. The researchers have not only shown that there have been no dramatic gains, but have rightly pointed out that you don't buy miracles with peanuts, that improvements are needed first in schools, the housing, the jobs and the resources available, and that the total impact of social policies is negatively discriminating. This has not been a popular message. The effort to evaluate social programmes has been run down, and few reports have been published.

The pressure to produce results can be illustrated by the Institute of Race Relations report *Colour and Citizenship*[21] discussed earlier. This was to have appeared as a series of studies with a summarising work by the directors of the whole study. But the furore caused by Enoch Powell's speeches on immigration persuaded Rose and Deakin to produce a report as quickly as possible as a corrective and a guide to policy-makers. There is no attempt in this book to conceal that the object was to remedy the social evil caused by treating coloured citizens as inferior, and the evidence produced was seen as a way of creating a more healthy environment for race relations.

Researchers always have to anticipate that their work will be given an unanticipated interpretation. Those who forwarded cultural deprivation as an explanation of low attainment were liberal in outlook and eager to help the poor. Later they were accused of being fascist for suggesting that the culture of the poor was inferior. Similarly the suggestion that different social classes employed different combinations of linguistic codes was seen as a start to help working class children in school, but was soon branded as a slur on the richness of their language. Barker Lunn, having produced a closely reasoned and neutral report on streaming in the primary school, met interpretations of the evidence that suggested that it had either not been read or not been understood.[22] Ford is mystified by the reception of her book on comprehensive schools.[23] She had every right to be, as the critics accused her of omitting that which was included and including that which was omitted. Yet this is the price that has to be paid for the producing research as an influence on policy. Only those who can stand the heat should get into the kitchen. This applies even though, as Barker Lunn concludes when looking back at the impact of her work, research cannot solve problems or answer questions.[24] These solutions and answers are the responsibility of politicians, administrators and practitioners working on the basis of all the evidence.

The relation of theory and practice

A recurrent theme in this book is that even the making of a simple fact requires reference to some theory that can give meaning to the observation or measurement. Just as concepts of space, time, causation and so on give meaning to observations of the physical world, so what we see of human behaviour or relationships becomes meaningful when referred to models of the social world. Social scientists have systematically developed models available for such interpretations. However fallible these prove to be, they are the basis for the claim to be able to produce insights. Without them the social scientist is on par with the informed lay observer. The scope of social research is therefore dependent on the quality of theory from which the researcher derives his procedures and to which he refers his results.

An illustration of this relevance of theory came from the involvement of social scientists in various Presidential Commissions set up to investigate important social problems in the United States.[25] Here the social scientists were on their home ground. But their concern for the status of evidence and their appreciation of the contrasting theoretical positions from which delinquency, drug addiction and other topical issues were viewed allowed the lawyers on the Commissions to dominate procedures. The main contribution that the sociologists involved saw themselves as making was to provide the concepts, the definitions and the contexts in which the problems were discussed. The reference back to theory seems to have inhibited the contribution of solutions, but helped provide a framework within which the complexities of the problems could be discussed. Significantly the major contribution of the social sciences to tackling the problems of the cities in the United States at this time was theoretical rather than empirical.[26] This was the hypothesis that delinquency resulted from blocked opportunities for working class youth. Many social programmes in the poverty programme were designed to remove a few of the blockages.

The danger of the continuous references to theory, whether intended or incidental, is that the evidence will be larded with jargon. Theory building often requires terms which may be derived from everyday use, but have to be defined within the context of the model being built. The layman is liable to see this as deliberate obscurantism. There is no doubt that jargon can give the impression of understanding where none exists. To explain the poor working habits and attainment of a group by reference to their lack of achievement motivation is merely to word the phenomenon differently, not to explain it. Unless achievement motivation is part of a developed conceptual framework there is no advance except the exercise of the worst form of professionalism. Yet this substitution of a convincing sounding term for a genuine explanation is very common.

The danger of jargon is that it separates the scientific community from its lay audience. The jargon used at conferences, in seminars, between colleagues, shows that you belong, overcomes nerves and is self-fulfilling. You learn it to be accepted and its use shows that you belong. This process is built into the accreditation of social scientists, for the language of a subject is sanctioned by the scientific community. This enables it to mark out its territory and to colonise that of others. But this linguistic imperialism is an academic game, not an essential part of theory building. Terms such as achievement motivation, linguistic deprivation, alienation, cultural hegemony, are concepts. They can help deepen understanding if they are part of a theoretical model, but their use without reference to it reduces them to Humpty Dumpty status. They mean only what the speaker wants them to mean.

The relation between expectations and outcomes

A frequent complaint about social scientific evidence from those who have to run affairs is that it never tells them what to do. Yet if it does the researcher is accused of trying to make policy. Researchers can confine themselves to evaluating the effects of policies. They can examine the processes through which policies are working, frustrated or deflected. But researchers are always uncovering the unintended and the uncomfortable. This is not just the product of a nose sharpened by subversive tendencies in sociology and its companion subjects. It is the consequence of the everyday equivalent of the reason why social science is not dependent on finding laws and causes. Just as most social scientists are reconciled that the social world is unsuitable for study by the methods of the natural sciences, so decision-makers usually recognise that they cannot legislate or execute with any certainty about the future course of events. The meaning given by humans to the social world around them happily frustrates both the scientifically-minded social scientist and the tidy-minded administrator. When the social researcher is given a brief to look at some aspect of the human condition, he will anticipate results because he will refer to available theories. But as he gives meaning to the data he collects, he will have to extend the brief. In the social world, problems are not self-contained. All that is required may be an account of the impact of setting up Educational Priority Areas and pumping in a few thousand pounds, but volume followed volume as the researchers tried to spell out the complexity of the situation for their sponsors. It was necessary to deepen the understanding of the context of the educational problem, to improve the questions asked before evaluation.

This complexity of social life and the impossibility of producing a brief that will enable the researcher to focus on a restricted problem, lies behind the complaint of the policy-maker that researchers do not deliver, and behind the researcher's complaint that he never really knows what he is supposed to be examining. If the brief could be precise there would be no point in the research. Inevitably, then, the social researcher gets involved in probing the gap between assumptions about real situations and the reality itself. It is this puncturing device that social scientists wield most effectively, because they are concerned with human beings who do convert the ideal into the practical, the simple into the complex and the administratively convenient into the bearable. The history of town planning, of high-rise flats and of motorways, and of the many other neat solutions to pressing social problems show that social factors are ignored at great cost. In these and many other cases social scientists, because they investigated the gap between the apparently reasonable policy and the apparently unreasonable response, were able to warn of problems to come.

There is also little doubt that this is an area where many social scientists are at home politically. This probing research into equality of opportunity, or income equalisation, or race prejudice, is inevitably loaded with the views of the researcher. There is little doubt that if the very influential research into the relation between social class and educational opportunity had been carried out by convinced fascists instead of reforming egalitarians, the results would have been very different. The evidence was reliable enough to convince. It demolished the assumption that equality of opportunity had been attained, and opened the way for reform within education even before the 1944 Education Act had been operative for a decade. In this country we tend to suspect left-wing bias in social scientific research. But in North America, the journal *The Public Interest* manifests a more right wing radicalism through its social science contributors. Targets such as affirmative discrimination and the effects of desegregating schools and busing against the wishes of blacks as well as whites, are shot at from the same theoretical base that is the launching pad for recommending such policies in a British journal such as *New Society*. Policies from left and from right have unintended effects. 'White Flight' may be unwelcome, but unless totalitarian policies are adopted there will always be such unintended responses. Significantly there is no social science as a subversive activity in totalitarian regimes.

This subversive role of social scientists is a problem for agencies that provide funds for research. The existence of a body such as the Social Science Research Council is a sign of the interest of government. But there has been concern over the pay-off from investment of public funds. The Rothschild report recommended that government departments should contract research so that it would have direct relevance to policy. The S.S.R.C. has shifted from responding to applications for research support from the academic world to initiation through earmarked money and the establishment of specialist centres and units. These are indications of interest but also of discontent. Such steps tend to be suspected by the research community who point to the need to improve the quality of the contributory subjects as a condition for better research. This case is grounded in the relation between theory and research practice. The sponsor's case is that the social sciences do not take sufficient interest in important, topical issues. Because of the differing views of the role of theory the views are not easily reconcilable.

The relation between central and marginal influence

Ministers such as Crosland or Boyle have described how they were influenced by social science while at the D.E.S.[27] Many social researchers feed evidence directly into central or local government, private business and public corporation. Other researchers influence policy through their affect on the media, through articles, books and conferences. When decisions are taken, any evidence, from any source, tends to be welcome. In education this evidence can come from inspectors, advisers, field officers and administrators who are usually professionals, and the teachers through their interest groups, as well as from researchers. All produce different evidence, slanted from different perspectives. This evidence does not produce the action. That is the result of a political act, and politicians at all levels are balancers of possibilities from all sources.

It is however only too easy to concentrate on the froth and fail to notice the body of social science. Historically it has helped in changing the way people understand the way they live together. Social scientists are always moving on to fresh research and to more sophisticated explanations. The folklore lags. But that folklore has still been changed. The theory of transmitted deprivation is now rejected by those now researching into poverty. But its acceptance by politicians and the public is an important milestone on the road from seeing poverty, crime, unemployment or poor educational attainment as the result of some personal, moral or inherited defect. It is an advance that social problems are now accepted as partly the consequences of forms of social organisation. Similar sequences have occurred in all the major lines of enquiry within the social sciences. Researchers working in the areas of human development, intelligence, socialisation, social class, sexual and ethnic differentiation have helped to remove much of the opacity out of everyday views of cause and effect in human affairs. They have shown that humans organise their own social problems and can hence solve them. The inevitability of mystical, moral and genetic explanations is removed and a search for a just organisation of human affairs can start. This book has dealt with contemporary controversies around the margins of social research. Below the limitations, the momentum of social research reduces the gap between reality and belief. This increases the possibility that the human condition can be improved by informed policies.

The exhilaration of, and motivation for, social science lies in this humane endeavour to improve the human lot. Social science is a haven for the curious, the alert, the detached and the nonconformist. This makes it even more urgent for social scientific communities to exercise discipline over individuals presenting new evidence. But the relevance of social science also requires not mystery but clarity in the picture presented to the public. Candour is needed to promote informed scepticism instead of naïve acceptance or rejection. This book was written to promote such scepticism. It should have been read in that spirit.

REFERENCES AND FURTHER READING

Controversy 1. Do teaching styles affect pupil progress?

1. S. N. Bennett, *Teaching Styles and Pupil Progress*, Open Books, 1976.
2. *The T.E.S.*, 30 April 1976, pp. 19–22.
3. See G. Bernbaum (ed.), *Schooling in Decline*, Macmillan, 1979.
4. *The T.E.S.*, 7 May 1976, p. 14.
5. G. W. Miller, letter to *The T.E.S.*, 14 May 1976, p. 15.
6. D. McIntyre, review of Bennett (above, n. 1) in *Brit. J. of Teacher Education*, 2 (3), 1977, pp. 291–7.
7. *The T.E.S.*, 30 April 1976, pp. 19–22.
8. *Ibid.*, p. 3.
9. J. Gray, 'What really goes on in class', in *The T.E.S.*, 7 May 1976, p. 24.
10. R. Sinha, letter to *The T.E.S.*, 7 May 1976, p. 24.
11. A. Clegg, letter to *The T.E.S.*, 14 May 1976, p. 15.
12. E. de Bono, letter to *The T.E.S.*, 14 May 1976, p. 15.
13. S. N. Bennett and N. Entwistle, 'Informal or formal: a reply', *The T.E.S.*, 21 May 1976, p. 2.
14. R. Walker, letter to *The T.E.S.*, 28 May 1976, p. 20.
15. J. M. Hughes, letter to *The T.E.S.*, 28 May 1976, p. 20.
16. *The T.E.S.*, 4 June 1976, pp. 17–19.
17. J. Gray, letter to *The T.E.S.*, 4 June 1976, p. 8.
18. J. Bruner, 'The Styles of Teaching', in *New Society*, 29 April 1976, pp. 223–5.
19. D. Satterly, letter to *New Society*, 6 May 1976, p. 315.
20. J. Gray and D. Satterly, 'A chapter of errors: teaching styles and pupil progress in retrospect', in *Ed. Res.* **19**, 1976, pp. 45–56.
21. S. N. Bennett and N. Entwistle, 'Rite and Wrong: a reply to "A Chapter of Errors",' in *Ed. Res.* **19**, 1976, pp. 217–22.
22. *Harvard Ed. Rev.* **47** (2), 1977, pp. 214–21.

Chapter 1. Scientific activity in theory and practice

1. P. Medawar, 'Is the scientific paper a fraud?' in D. Edge (ed.), *Experiment*, B.B.C., 1964, pp. 7–12.
2. J. E. Myers, 'Unleashing the untrained: some observations of student ethnographers', *Human Organization*, Summer 1969, pp. 155–60.

3. C. H. McCaghy and J. K. Skipper, 'Lesbian behaviour as an adaptation to the occupation of stripping', *Social Problems*, Fall 1969, pp. 262–70; and J. K. Skipper and C. H. McCaghy, 'Stripteasers: the anatomy and career contingencies of a deviant occupation', *Social Problems*, Winter 1970, pp. 391–405.
4. But see P. E. Hammond, *Sociologists at Work*, Basic Books, 1964.
5. J. S. Coleman, in Hammond, *op. cit.*, pp. 184–211. See also C. Bell and H. Newby (eds.), *Doing Sociological Research*, Allen & Unwin, 1977. And M. Shipman (ed.), *The Organisation and Impact of Social Research*, Routledge & Kegan Paul, 1976.
6. H. Blumer, *An Appraisal of Thomas and Znaniecki's 'The Polish Peasant in Europe and America'*, Social Science Research Council, p. 83 and pp. 103–6.
7. *Children and Their Primary Schools* (Plowden Report), H.M.S.O., 1966, pp. 189–202.
8. W. I. Beveridge, *The Art of Scientific Investigation*, Heinemann, 1950, pp. 27–44.
9. B. Barber and R. Short, 'The case of the floppy-eared rabbits: an instance of serendipity gained and serendipity lost', *American Journal of Sociology*, 1958, pp. 128–36.
10. E. Garfield, 'Negative science and "The Outlook for the Flying Machine"', *Current Contents* **26**, June 27, 1977, p. 13.
11. *Ibid.*, pp. 17–22.
12. *Ibid.*, p. 8.

Controversy 2. What do school leavers think about schools?

1. P. Willis, *Learning to Labour*, Saxon House, 1978.
2. D. E. Scharff, 'Aspects of the transition from school to work', in J. M. M. Hill and D. E. Scharff, *Between Two Worlds*, Careers Consultants Ltd., 1976, pp. 66–332.
3. Willis, *op. cit.*, p. 11.
4. Scharff, *op. cit.*, pp. 235–54.

Chapter 2. Social science

1. Scharff, *op. cit.* (Controversy 2, n.2).
2. Willis, *op. cit.* (Controversy 2, n.1).
3. Coleman, *op. cit.* (ch.1, n.5).
4. E. Glueck and S. Glueck, *Unraveling Juvenile Delinquency*, Commonwealth Fund, 1950.
5. E. M. Lemert, *Social Pathology*, McGraw-Hill, 1951.
6. H. Becker, *Outsiders*, Free Press, 1963.
7. G. H. Bantock, 'Literature and the Social Sciences', paper read at the Annual Conference of the *British Sociological Association*, 1970.
8. S. Schoeffler, *The Failures of Economics: a diagnostic study*, Harvard University Press, 1955, pp. 40–1.
9. H. P. Rickman, *Understanding and the Social Sciences*, Heinemann, 1967, pp. 24–36.

10. R. Harré and P. F. Secord, *The Explanation of Social Behaviour*, Blackwell, 1972.
11. A. V. Cicourel, *Method and Measurement in Sociology*, Free Press, 1964.
12. B. G. Glaser and A. L. Strauss, *The Discovery of Grounded Theory*, Weidenfeld and Nicolson, 1968.

Controversy 3. Should scientists investigate sensitive social problems?

1. A. R. Jensen, 'How much can we boost IQ and scholastic achievement?', *Harvard Ed. Rev.*, Winter 1969, pp. 1–123. For a similar British view see C. Burt, 'Intelligence and heredity', *New Scientist*, 1 May 1969, pp. 226–8.
2. *Harvard Ed. Rev.*, Spring 1969.
3. *Harvard Ed. Rev.*, Summer 1969, pp. 449–83.
4. W. F. Brazziel, 'A letter from the South', *Harvard Ed. Rev*, Spring 1969, p. 348.
5. *Ibid.*
6. M. K. Barry, letter to *New Society*, 24 June 1971, p. 1108.
7. Brazziel, *op. cit.*
8 A. R. Jensen, 'Do schools cheat minority children?', *Ed. Res.*, Vol. 14, no. 1, Nov. 1971, pp. 3–28. This article was advertised to appear in *Educational Research* for November 1971, after this typescript was completed and after the criticisms of the NFER appeared.
9. M. Morris, quoted in B. Hill, 'NFER attacked over Jensen article', *The T.E.S.*, 17 Sept. 1971, p. 5.
10. D. Pidgeon, quoted in Hill *ibid*. See also letters to *The T.E.S.*, 1 Oct. 1971, p. 20.
11. H. J. Eysenck, *Race, Intelligence and Education*, M. Temple Smith, 1971.
12. See particularly *New Society*, 24 June 1971 and 1 July 1971, pp. 29–30.
13. L. Hudson, Review of Eysenck's *Race, Intelligence and Education*, *New Society*, 1 July 1971, pp. 29–30.
14. W. F. Bodmer and L. L. Cavalli-Sforza, 'Intelligence and race', *Scientific American*, Oct. 1970, pp. 19–29.
15. As a moderate illustration see H. Gans, 'Where sociologists have failed', in N. K. Denzin, *The Values of Social Science*, Trans-action Books, 1970, pp. 83–6.
16. W. Bodmer, 'Genetics and intelligence: the race argument', in A. H. Halsey (ed.), *Heredity and Environment*, Methuen, 1977, p. 319.
17. National Union of Teachers, *Race, Education, Intelligence*, 1978.
18. H. Eysenck and S. Rose, 'Race, intelligence and education', *New Community* 7, 2, Summer 1979, pp. 278–83.
19. L. S. Hearnshaw, *Cyril Burt: Psychologist*, Hodder and Stoughton, 1979.
20. N.U.T., *op. cit.*
21. N.U.T., *op. cit.*, p. 15.
22. M. D. Shipman, 'The limits of positive discrimination', in M. Marland, *Education for the Inner City*, Heinemann, 1980, pp. 69–92.

Chapter 3. Questions of author, subject and date.

1. C. Lacey. 'Problems of sociological fieldwork: a review of the methodology of

"Hightown Grammar"', in M. D. Shipman, *The Organisation and Impact of Social Research*, Routledge & Kegan Paul, 1976, pp. 63–88.

2. R. Blackburn, 'A brief guide to bourgeois ideology', in A. Cockburn and R. Blackburn, *Student Power*, Penguin, 1969, pp. 199–200.

3. A. V. Gouldner, 'Anti-Minotaur: the myth of value-free sociology', *Social Problems* **9**, 1962, pp. 199–213.

4. C. W. Mills, *The Sociological Imagination*, Oxford University Press, 1959, pp. 50–75.

5. W. G. Runciman, 'Thinking by Numbers', *The T.E.S.*, 6 Aug. 1971, pp. 943–4.

6. Gouldner, *op. cit.*

7. F. J. Roethlisberger and W. J. Dickson, *Management and the Worker*, Wiley, 1939.

8. R. Lippitt and R. K. White, 'An experimental study of leadership and group life', in H. P. Proshansky and B. Seidenberg, *Basic Studies in Social Psychology*, Holt, Rinehart and Winston, 1965, pp. 523–37.

9. B. R. McCandless, *Children: Behaviour and Development*, Holt, Rinehart and Winston, 1967, p. 564.

10. J. Platt, *The Realities of Research*, University of Sussex Press, 1976.

11. Bell and Newby, *op. cit.* (ch.1, n.5).

12. Shipman, *op. cit.* (ch.1, n.5).

13. Hammond, *op. cit.* (ch.1, n.4).

14. R. R. Dale, '"Mixed or single-sex school": a comment on a research study', in M. D. Shipman, *op. cit.* (ch.1, n.4), pp. 120–38.

15. J. and E. Newson, 'Parental roles and social contexts', in M. D. Shipman, *op. cit* (ch. 1, n.5), pp. 22–48.

16. C. Bell, 'Reflections on the Banbury Restudy', in Bell and Newby, *op. cit.* (ch.1, n.5), pp. 47–107.

17. J. Ford, 'Facts, evidence and rumour: a rational reconstruction of "Social Class and the Comprehensive School"', in Shipman, *op. cit.* (ch. 1, n.5), pp. 51–62.

18. J. W. B. Douglas, 'The use and abuse of national cohorts', in Shipman, *op. cit.* (ch. 1, n.5), pp. 3–21.

19. Dale, *op. cit.* p.121.

20. See G. Hoinville and R. Jowell, 'What happened in the election?', *New Society*, 2 July 1970, pp. 12–14.

21. J. Hemming, *Problems of Adolescent Girls*, Heinemann, 1960.

22. T. Tapper, *Young People and Society*, Faber, 1971.

23. D. H. Hargreaves, *Social Relations in a Secondary School*, Routledge & Kegan Paul, 1967.

24. J. W. B. Douglas and J. M. Blomfield, *Children Under Five*, Allen & Unwin, 1958.

25. J. W. B. Douglas, *The Home and the School*, MacGibbon & Kee, 1964.

26. J. W. B. Douglas, *All Our Future*, Davies, 1968.

27. W. Brandis and D. Henderson, *Social Class Language and Communication*, Routledge & Kegan Paul, 1970.

28. E. H. Carr, *What is History?*, Penguin, 1964, pp. 20–30.

29. M. Mead, *Coming of Age in Samoa*, Cape, 1929; Penguin 1943.

30. M. Mead, *Growing Up in New Guinea*, Routledge & Kegan Paul, 1931, Penguin 1942.

31. Li An-Che, 'Zuni. Some observations and queries', *American Anthropology* **39**, 1937, pp. 62–76.

32. E. H. Sutherland, *White Collar Crime*, Holt, Rinehart & Winston, 1949. First article was 'White collar criminality', *Am. Soc. Rev.*, Feb. 1940, pp. 1–12.
33. See, for example, E. M. Lemert, *Human Deviance, Social Problems and Social Control*, Prentice-Hall, 1967.
34. I. L. Horowitz, *The Rise and Fall of Project Camelot*, Massachusetts Institute of Technology Press, 1967; see also G. Sjoberg, *Ethics, Politics and Social Research*, Routledge & Kegan Paul, 1969, pp. 141–61.
35. W. O. Hagstrom, *The Scientific Community*, Basic Books, 1965, pp. 69–104.
36. R. K. Merton, 'Priorities in scientific discovery', in B. Barber and W. Hirsch, *The Sociology of Science*, Free Press, 1962, pp. 447–85.
37. I L. Horowitz, 'The natural history of "Revolution in Brazil"; a biography of a book', in Sjoberg, *op. cit.*, pp. 198–224.
38. J. Ford, *Social Class and the Comprehensive School*, Routledge & Kegan Paul, 1969, pp. vii and viii.
39. Horowitz, *The Rise and Fall of Project Camelot, op. cit.*
40. Z. A. Medvedev, *The Rise and Fall of T. D. Lysenko*, Columbia University Press, 1969.
41. See *The T.E.S.*, 7 Aug, 1970, p. 1, and *The T.E.S.*, 21 Aug. 1970, p. 10.
42. J. D. Watson, *The Double Helix*, Weidenfeld & Nicolson, 1968.
43. J. S. Weiner, *The Piltdown Forgery*, Oxford University Press, 1955.
44. D. S. Greenberg, *The Politics of American Science*, Penguin, 1969, pp. 219–60.

Controversy 4. Can teachers act Pygmalion in the classroom?

1. R. Rosenthal and L. Jacobson, *Pygmalion in the Classroom*, Holt, Rinehart and Winston, 1968.
2. J. D. Elashoff and R. E. Snow, *Pygmalion Reconsidered*, C. A. Jones, 1971.
3. *Ibid.*, pp. 8–18. See also R. L. Thorndike, 'Review of Pygmalion in the Classroom', *American Education Research Journal*, 5, 1968, pp. 708–11.
4. Elashoff and Snow, *op. cit.*
5. Thorndike, *op. cit.*
6. R. E. Snow, 'Unfinished Pygmalion', *Contemporary Psychology*, **14**, 1969, pp. 197–9.
7. Elashoff and Snow, *op. cit.* See also R. Rosenthal, 'The Pygmalion effect lives', *Psychology Today*, 7, 4, 1973, pp. 56–63.
8. J. P. Barker and J. L. Crist, 'Teacher expectations: a review of the literature', in Elashoff and Snow, *op. cit.*, pp. 48–64.

Chapter 4. Sampling

1. Blumer, *op. cit.* (ch.1, n.6).
2. Schools Council, *Enquiry Number 1, Young School Leavers*, H.M.S.O., 1968.
3. J. H. Goldthorpe *et al.*, *The Affluent Worker: industrial attitudes and behaviour*, Cambridge University Press, 1968.
4. J. F. Floud, A. H. Halsey and F. M. Martin, *Social Class and Educational Opportunity*, Heinemann, 1956.
5. B. Jackson and D. Marsden, *Education and the Working Class*, Routledge & Kegan Paul, 1962.
6. Hargreaves, *op. cit.* (ch.3, n.23).

7. J. Wakeford, *The Cloistered Elite*, Macmillan, 1969.
8. M. Young and P. Willmott, *Family and Kinship in East London*, Routledge & Kegan Paul, 1957, Penguin, 1962; and *Family and Class in a London Suburb*, Routledge & Kegan Paul, 1960, Penguin, 1964.
9. M. D. Shipman, 'Environmental influences on response to questionnaires', *British Journal of Educational Psychology*, 1967.
10. Wakeford, *op. cit.*
11. S. Isaacs, *Social Development in Young Children*, Routledge & Kegan Paul, 9th impression, 1964.
12. A. C. Kinsey *et al.*, *Sexual Behaviour in the Human Female*, W. B. Saunders, 1953, pp. 58–100.
13. T. Veness, *School Leavers*, Methuen, 1962, pp. 1–25.
14. M. Phillips, *Small Social Groups in England*, Methuen, 1965, pp. 3–19.
15. Hemming, *op. cit* (ch.3, n.21).
16. For this and other blunders, see L. Rogers, *The Pollsters*, Knopf, 1949.
17. J. Gabriel, *The Emotional Problems of the Teacher in the Classroom*, F. W. Cheshire (Melbourne), 1957.
18. F. Musgrove, *Youth and the Social Order*, Routledge & Kegan Paul, 1964.
19. J. Newson and E. Newson, *Infant Care in an Urban Community*, Allen & Unwin, 1968.
20. P. Willmott, *Adolescent Boys of East London*, Routledge & Kegan Paul, 1966.
21. Douglas, *op. cit.*, three books (ch.3, nn.24,25,26).
22. F. W. Miller *et al.*, *Growing up in Newcastle upon Tyne*, Oxford University Press, 1960.
23. T. W. Adorno *et al.*, *The Authoritarian Personality*, Harper Bros., 1960. See also Chapter 7. See also H. H. Hyman and P. B. Sheatsley, 'The authoritarian personality – a methodological critique', in R. Christie and M. Jahoda, *Studies in the Scope and Method of 'The Authoritarian Personality'*, Free Press, 1954, pp. 50–122.

Controversy 5. Have we underestimated the reasoning power of young children?

1. *Children and their Primary Schools* (Plowden Report), H.M.S.O., 1966, p. 142.
2. For examples, see S. and C. Modgil, *Piagetian Research. Compilation and Commentary*, vols.1–8, N.F.E.R., 1976.
3. M. Donaldson, *Children's Minds*, Fontana/Collins, 1978.
4. For example, M. Brearley and E. Hitchfield, *A Teacher's Guide to Reading Piaget*, Routledge & Kegan Paul, 1966.
5. P. E. Bryant and T. Trabasso, 'Transitive inferences and memory in young children', *Nature* 232, 13 Aug. 1971, pp. 456–8.
6. See *The Observer* 22 Aug. 1971, p. 4, and 12 Sept. 1971, p. 7.
7. See *Daily Telegraph*, 23 Aug. 1971. For an account of the press reports following the original article in the *Observer* on 22 Aug. 1971, see *The T.E.S.*, 10 Sept. 1971, p. 80.
8. *The Observer*, 12 Sept. 1971, p. 7.
9. E. Duckworth, 'Either we're too early and they can't learn it or we're too late and they know it already: the dilemma of "Applying Piaget"', *Harvard Ed. Rev.* 49, 3, 1979, pp. 297–313.
10. See G. Matthews, 'Piaget and his critics: part two', *The T.E.S.*, 10 Sept. 1971, p. 4.

Chapter 5. Studies based on observation

1. R. Rosenthal and K. L. Fode, 'The effect of experimenter bias on the performance of albino rats', *Behavioural Science*, 1963, pp. 183–9.
2. I. Firth, 'N-rays — ghost of a scandal past', *New Scientist*, 25 Dec. 1969, pp. 642–3. H. J. Eysenck, *Fact and Fiction in Psychology*, Penguin, 1965, pp. 127–30. I. J. Good, *The Scientist Speculates*, Heinemann, 1962, Index.
3. A. J. Reiss, 'Stuff and Nonsense about social surveys and observations', in H. S. Becker *et al.*, *Institution and the Person*, Aldine Press, 1968, pp. 351–67.
4. R. Frankenberg, 'Participant observation', *New Society*, 7 March 1963, pp. 22–3.
5. H. Gans, 'The participant observer as a human being', in Becker *et al.*, *op. cit.*, pp. 300–17.
6. A. Vidich, J. Bensman and M. R. Stein (eds.), *Reflections on Community Studies*, Wiley, 1964.
7. J. R. Seeley, 'Crestwood Heights: intellectual and libidinal dimensions of research', in Vidich *et al.*, *op. cit.*, pp. 157–206.
8. M. R. Stein, 'The eclipse of community: some glances at the education of a sociologist', in Vidich *et al.*, *op. cit.*, pp. 207–32.
9. K. H. Wolff, 'Surrender and community study: the study of Loma', in Vidich *et al.*, *op. cit.*, pp. 233–64.
10. W. F. Whyte, *Street Corner Society*, University of Chicago Press, enlarged edition, 1954, pp. 279–360.
11. A. J. Vidich, 'Freedom and responsibility in research: a rejoinder', *Human Organization*, Spring 1960, pp. 3–4.
12. I. Festinger *et al.*, *When Prophecy Fails*, University of Minnesota Press, 1956.
13. R. F. Bales, *Interaction Process Analysis*, Addison-Wesley, 1950.
14. C. Madge and H. Jennings, *May the Twelfth, Mass Observation Day Surveys*, Faber, 1937.
15. H. S. Becker, 'Problems of inference and proof in participant observation', *American Sociological Review* 23, 1958, pp. 652–60.
16. O. Lewis, *Life in a Mexican Village: Tepoztlan Restudied*, Univ. of Illinois Press, 1951.
17. R. Redfield, *Tepoztlan, A Mexican Village: A Study of Folk Life*. Univ. of Chicago Press, 1930.
18. M. Avila, *Tradition and Growth*, Univ. of Chicago Press, 1969.
19. R. Redfield, *The Primitive World and its Transformations*, Penguin, 1968, p.158.

Controversy 6. Do the public want religious education in state schools?

1. R. Goldman, 'Do we want our children taught about God?', *New Society*, 27 May 1965, pp. 8-10.
2. British Humanist Society, *N.O.P. Survey*, 1969.
3. Schools Council, *op. cit.* (ch.4, n.2).
4. *The Fourth R* (The Durham Report), S.P.C.K., 1970, pp. 96–7.

Chapter 6 Information through asking questions

1. R. Jowell and G. Hoinville, 'Opinion polls tested', *New Society*, 7 Aug. 1969, pp. 206–7.
2. R. Blackburn, 'A brief guide to bourgeois ideology', in A. Cockburn and R. Blackburn, *Student Power*, Penguin 1969, pp. 199–200.
3. N. Gross, W. S. Mason and A. W. McEachern, *Explorations in Role Analysis*, Wiley, 1966.
4. S. L. Payne, *The Art of Asking Questions*, Princeton University Press, 1951.
5. A. Smithers and S. Carlisle, 'Reluctant teachers', *New Society*, 5 March 1970, pp. 391–2.
6. Shipman, *op. cit.* (ch.4, n.9).
7. Adorno, *op. cit.* (ch.4, n.23) and Hyman and Sheatsley, *op. cit.* (ch.4, n.23).
8. E. Frenkel-Brunswick, in Hyman and Sheatsley, *ibid.*, pp. 226–75.
9. E. Z. Vogt and R. Hyman, *Water Witching U.S.A.*, University of Chicago Press, 1959, pp. 92–9.
10. Kinsey, *op. cit.* (ch.4, n.12).
11. Government Social Survey, *Handbook for Interviewers*, H.M.S.O.
12. C. A. Moser, *Survey Methods in Social Investigation*, Heinemann, 1958, pp. 193–4.
13. J. Durbin and A. Stuart, 'Differences in response rates of experienced and inexperienced interviewers', *J. Roy. Statistical Society*, 1951, pp. 163–205.
14. F. Zweig, *The Quest for Fellowship*, Heinemann, 1965, pp. 1–33.
15. J. Rich, *Interviewing Children and Adolescents*, Macmillan, 1968.
16. J. Holt, 'Ask a silly question', *The T.E.S.*, 17 July 1970, p. 4.
17. P. Townsend, *The Last Refuge*, Routledge & Kegan Paul, 1962, pp. 3–16; see also P. Townsend, *The Family Life of Old People*, Routledge & Kegan Paul, 1957, pp. 3–10.
18. Kinsey, *op. cit.* (ch.3, n.12).
19. See N. K. Denzin, *The Research Art in Sociology*, Butterworth, 1970, pp. 122–43.
20. Newson and Newson, *op. cit.* (ch.3, n.15).

Controversy 7. To stream or unstream?

1. J. C. Barker Lunn, *Streaming in the Primary School*, N.F.E.R., 1970.
2. I. E. Finch, 'A study of the personal and social consequence of groups of secondary schooling of the experience of different methods of allocation within secondary courses', M.A. thesis, University of London, 1954.
3. W. G. A. Rudd, 'The psychological effects of streaming by attainment with special reference to a group of selected children', *B.J.E.P.*, 1956, pp. 47–60.
4. J. S. Blandford, 'Standardised tests in junior schools with special reference to the effects of streaming on the consistency of results', *B.J.E.P.*, 1958, pp. 170–3.
5. J. M. Morris, *Reading in the Primary School*, N.F.E.R., 1959.
6. J. C. Daniels, 'Some effects of segregation and streaming on the intellectual and scholastic development of Junior School children', Ph.D. thesis, University of Nottingham, 1959.
7. A. Yates and D. A. Pidgeon, 'The effects of streaming', *Ed. Res.*, Nov. 1959.
8. B. Simon, 'Non-streaming in the Junior School', *Forum*, 1964.
9. Douglas, *op. cit.* (ch.3, n.8).

10. B. Jackson, *Streaming*, Routledge & Kegan Paul, 1964.
11. Barker Lunn, *op. cit.*
12. M. Goldberg *et al.*, *Effects of Ability Grouping*, Columbia University Press, 1966.
13. R. B. Ekstrom, *Experimental Studies of Homogeneous Grouping: a review of the literature*, Princeton University Press, 1959.
14. See S. Maclure, *Education*, 2 May 1969.
15. A. Yates, *Grouping in Education*, Hamburg, Unesco Institute for Education, 1966, pp. 131–2. See also T. Husen, *International Study of Achievement in Mathematics*, Stockholm, Almquist & Wicksell, 1967.
16. Surrey Educational Research Association, *To Stream or not to Stream*, 1968.
17. J. Barker Lunn, 'Streaming in the Primary School', in Shipman, *op. cit.* (ch.1, n.5), pp. 91–119.

Chapter 7. Experiments

1. D. H. Hargreaves, S. K. Hestor and F. J. Mellor, *Deviance in Classrooms*, Routledge & Kegan Paul, 1975.
2. M. Sherif, *The Psychology of Social Norms*, Harper and Row, 1936.
3. Glueck and Glueck, *op. cit.* (ch.2, n.4).
4. See Controversy 7.
5. See Controversy 9.
6. See for example, J. Gray, 'Positive discrimination in education: a review of the British experience', *Policy and Politics*, **4**, 2, 1975, pp. 85–111.
7. Roethlisberger and Dickson, *op. cit.* (ch.3, n.7).
8. A. Carey, 'The Hawthorne Studies: a radical analysis', *Am. Soc. Rev.*, 1967, pp. 403–16.
9. M. Young and P. McGeeney, *Learning Begins at Home*, Routledge & Kegan Paul, 1968, pp. 87–106
10. H. G. Canady, 'The effect of "Rapport" on the I.Q.: a new approach to the problem of racial psychology', *J. Negro Studies*, 1936, pp. 208–19.
11. A. Rabin, W. Nelson and M. Clark, 'Rorschach content as a function of perceptual experience and sex of examiner', *Journal of Clinical Psychology*, 1954, pp. 188–90.
12. J. Masling, 'The influence of situational and interpersonal variables in projective testing', *Psychol. Bulletin*, 1960. pp. 65–85.
13. J. Masling, 'Effect of warm and cold interaction on the administration and scoring of an intelligence test', *Journal of Consulting Psychology*, 1959, pp. 336–41.
14. M. T. Orne, 'On the social psychology of the psychological experiment', *Am. Psych.*, 1962, pp. 776–83
15. N. Friedman, *The Social Nature of Psychological Research*, Basic Books, 1967, contains many examples of this type of confusion.
16. R. Rosenthal, *Experimenter Effects in Behavioural Research*, Appleton-Century-Crofts, 1966.
17. Friedman, *op. cit.*, pp. 33–69.
18. M. T. Orne, 'The nature of hypnosis: artifact and essence', *Journal of Abnormal Social Psychology*, 1959, pp. 277–99.

Controversy 8. The Reformation and the schools

1. A. F. Leach, *The Schools of Medieval England*, Methuen, 1916.
2. J. Simon, 'A. F. Leach of the Reformation, I', *B.J.E.S.*, May 1955, pp. 128–143 and 'II', *British Journal of Educational Studies*. Nov. 1955, pp. 32–48; and *Education and Society in Tudor England*, Cambridge University Press, 1966.
3. W. N. Chaplin, 'A. F. Leach: a re-appraisal', *B.J.E.S.*, May 1963, pp. 99–124.
4. W. K. Jordan, *Philanthropy in England 1480–1660*, Allen & Unwin, 1959.
5. F. J. Fisher, Book review, *Brit. J. Soc.*, March 1960, pp. 188–9.

Chapter 8. Documents and other unobtrusive measures.

1. A. V. Cicourel, *The Social Organization of Juvenile Justice*, Wiley, 1967.
2. L. Gottschalk, C. Kluckhohn and R. Angell, 'The use of personal documents in history', *Anthropology and Sociology*, S.S.R.C. 1951, pp. 3–75.
3. Home Office, *Report of the Departmental Committee on Criminal Statistics* (Chairman: M. W. Perks), Cmnd. 3448, 1967.
4. H. Mannheim, *Comparative Criminology*, Vol. 1, Routledge & Kegan Paul, 1965, p. 114.
5. Home Office, *op. cit.* pp. 10–11.
6. Mannheim, *op. cit.* pp. 98–118, for a discussion of the reliability of statistics.
7. A. V. Cicourel, *The Social Organization of Juvenile Justice*, Wiley, 1967.
8. *Ibid.*, pp. 26–9. See also J. Kitsuse and A. V. Cicourel, 'A note on the uses of official statistics', *Social Problems*, 1963, pp. 131–9.
9. Cicourel, *op. cit.*
10. W. I. Thomas and F. Znaniecki, *The Polish Peasant in Europe and America*, 2 volume edition, 1927.
11. Blumer, *op. cit.* (ch.1, n.6), pp. 28–53.
12. *Ibid.*, pp. 74–6 and 109–10.
13. *Ibid.*
14. E. J. Webb *et al.*, *Unobtrusive Measures*, Rand McNally, 1966.

Controversy 9. Terrorist or Resistance Fighter? The case of the football hooligan

1. J. A. Harrington, *Soccer Hooliganism*, J. Wright, 1968.
2. See Sports Council and S.S.R.C., *Public Disorder and Sporting Events*, Social Science Research Council, 1978.
3. S. Hall, 'The treatment of "football hooliganism" in the press', in R. Ingham *et al.*, *'Football Hooliganism': the wider context*, Inter-Action Inprint, 1978.
4. I. Taylor, '"Football Mad". A speculative sociology of football hooliganism', in E. Dunning, *The Sociology of Sport*, Cass, 1971, pp. 352–77. See also I. Taylor, 'Hooligans: soccer's resistance movement', *New Society*, 7 Aug. 1969, pp. 204–6.
5. J. Clarke, 'Football and working class fans: tradition and change', in R. Ingham, *op. cit.*, pp. 37–60.
6. Taylor, *op. cit.*, (1971).

200   *The Limitations of Social Research*

7. P. Marsh, *Aggro. The Illusion of Violence*, Dent, 1978, p. 147.
8. Sports Council and S.S.R.C., *op. cit.*

Chapter 9. Interpretative social science and ethnography

1. A. Schutz, 'Concept and theory formation in the social sciences', in J. Bynner and K. M. Stribley, *Social Research: Principles and Procedures*, Longman, 1978, pp. 25–36.
2. J. Young, 'The role of the police as amplifiers of delinquency, negotiators of reality and translators of fantasy', in S. Cohen (ed.), *Images of Deviance*, Penguin, 1971.
3. *Ibid.*
4. S. Henry, *The Hidden Economy*, Robertson, 1978.
5. J. Ditton, *Part-Time Crime: An Ethnography of Fiddling and Pilferage*, Macmillan, 1977.
6. G. Mars, 'Dock Pilferage', in P. Rock and M. McIntosh (eds.), *Deviance and Control*, Tavistock, 1974.
7. C. Fletcher, *Beneath the Surface*, Routledge & Kegan Paul, 1974.
8. See P. Rock, *The Making of Symbolic Interactionism*, Macmillan, 1979. See also N. K. Denzin, 'The logic of naturalistic inquiry', in Bynner and Stribley, *op. cit.*, pp. 37–43.
9. H. S. Becker, 'Problems in the publication of field studies', in Vidich, Bensman and Stein, *op. cit.* (ch.5, n.6), pp. 267–84.
10. G. H. Mead, *Mind, Self and Society*, Univ. of Chicago Press, 1934.
11. H. Blumer, 'Sociological implications of the thought of G. H. Mead', *Amer. J. of Soc.*, 71, 1966, pp. 535–48.
12. Open University, *School and Society: A Sociological Reader*, Routledge & Kegan Paul, 1971.
13. M. F. D. Young (ed.), *Knowledge and Control: New Directions for the Sociology of Education*, Collier-Macmillan, 1971.
14. G. Esland, 'Teaching and learning as the organization of knowledge', in Young, *op. cit.*, pp. 70–115.
15. N. Keddie, 'Classroom knowledge', in Young, *op. cit.*, pp. 133–160.
16. G. Bernbaum, *Knowledge and Ideology in the Sociology of Education*, Macmillan, 1977.
17. Hargreaves, *op. cit.* (ch.3, n.23).
18. Hargreaves, Hestor and Mellor, *op. cit.* (ch.7, n.1).
19. P. Marsh, E. Rosser and R. Harré, *The Rules of Disorder*, Routledge & Kegan Paul, 1978, pp. 30–57.
20. See G. Easthope, *History of Social Research Methods*, Longman, 1974, pp. 61–7 and 99–100.
21. Harré and Secord, *op. cit.* (ch.2, n.10).
22. R. Harré, 'The constructive role of models', in L. Collins (ed.), *The Use of Models in the Social Sciences*, Tavistock, 1976.
23. Marsh, Rosser and Harré, *op. cit.*
24. M. D. Shipman, D. Bolam and D. Jenkins, *Inside a Curriculum Project*, Methuen, 1974.

25. Goffman, *op. cit.* (ch.2, n.11).
26. H. Garfinkel, *Studies in Ethnomethodology*, Prentice Hall, 1967, p. 174.
27. A. Gouldner, *The Coming Crisis in American Sociology*, Basic Books, 1970, pp. 378–90.
28. B. Malinowski, *Argonauts of the Western Pacific*, Routledge & Kegan Paul, 1922.
29. F. M. Thrasher, 'How to study the boys' gang in the open', *J. of Educ. Soc.*, **1**, 1928.
30. P. Willis, *Profane Culture*, Routledge & Kegan Paul, 1978.
31. J. Patrick, *A Glasgow Gang Observed*, Eyre Methuen, 1973.
32. W. F. Whyte, *Street Corner Society*, Univ. of Chicago Press, 1943.
33. N. Anderson, *The Hobo*, Univ. of Chicago Press, 1923.
34. C. R. Shaw, *The Jack Roller*, Univ. of Chicago Press, 1967.
35. *Op. cit.* (nn. 4, 5 and 6).
36. *Op. cit.* (Controversy 2, n.1)
37. Willis, *op. cit.*
38. F. Musgrove, 'Review of "Profane Culture"3', *Research in Education*, **20**, 1979, pp. 93–96.
39. Hargreaves, *op. cit.* (ch.3, n.23).
40. Lacey, *op. cit.* (ch.3, n.1).
41. Gabriel, *op. cit.* (ch.4, n.17).
42. Hemming, *op. cit.* (ch.3, n.21).
43. Marsh, Rosser and Harré, *op. cit.*
44. M. D. Shipman, *The Sociology of the School*, 2nd edn, 1975.
45. N. K. Denzin, *op. cit.* (ch.6, n.19).

Controversy 10. The priority given to reducing the size of school classes

1. C. Fleming, 'Class size as a variable in the teaching situation', *Ed. Res.*, Feb. 1959, pp. 35–48.
2. P. Rossi, 'Evaluating social action programmes', in N. Denzin, *The Values of Social Science*, Trans-action Books, 1970, pp. 89–90.
3. P. J. Powell, *Class Size: a Summary of Research*, Educational Research Inc., 1978.
4. T. Husen, *International Study of Achievement in Mathematics*, Almquist and Wicksell, Stockholm, 1967, pp. 277–83.
5. A. Little and J. Russell, paper read at the UK Reading Association Conference, 1971: see *The T.E.S.*, 30 Sept. 1971, p. 5.
6. Morris, *op. cit.* (Contro 6, n.5), pp. 93–5 and 223–4.
7. R. Davie, 'The child, the school and the home'. Paper read at the Annual meeting of the British Association for the Advancement of Science (Education section), 3 Sept. 1970; paper kindly provided by the author.
8. C. Burstall, 'Time to mend the nets: a commentary on the outcomes of class-size research', *Trends*, **3**, 1979, pp. 27–33.
9. *Children and their Primary Schools* (Plowden Report), *op. cit.* (ch.1, n.7), pp. 279–82

Chapter 10. The preparation and presentation of the evidence

1. I. Miles and J. Irvine, 'The critique of official statistics', in J. Irvine, I. Miles and J. Evans, *Demystifying Social Statistics*, Pluto Press, 1979, pp. 113–29.
2. Newsom Report, *op. cit.*, and Robbins Report, *op. cit.* (ch.3, nn.29, 28).
3. See, for example, J. R. Amos *et al.*, *Statistical Concepts*, Harper & Row, 1965.
4. For example, W. J. Reichmann, *Use and Abuses of Statistics*, Methuen, 1961.
5. For example, H. Miner, 'Researchmanship: the feedback of expertise', *Human Organisation*, Spring 1960, pp. 1–3.
6. S. Labovitz, 'The nonutility of significance tests: the significance of tests of significance reconsidered', *Pacific Sociological Review*, 1970, pp. 141–8.
7. D. Gold, 'Statistical tests and substantive significance', *American Sociologist*, 1969, pp. 42–6.
8. H. C. Selvin, 'A critique of tests of significance in survey research', *Am. Soc. Rev.*, 1957, pp. 519–27.
9. J. S. Coleman, letter, *American Journal of Sociology*, 1958, pp. 56–60.
10. S. F. Camilleri, 'Theory, probability and induction in social research', *Am. Soc. Rev.*, 1962, pp. 170–8.
11. E. Gowers, *The Complete Plain Words*, Penguin edn, 1962, p.69.
12. Extracted from A. Kohn, 'Principles and methods of obscuratism', *New Scientist*, 29 Jan. 1970.
13. B. Cane and C. Schroeder, *The Teacher and Research*, N.F.E.R., 1970, p.39.
14. V. Southgate and G. R. Roberts, *Reading – Which Approach?*, University of London Press, 1970.
15. D. Lawton, *Social Class, Language and Education*, Routledge & Kegan Paul, 1968, pp. 77–102; see 'Comment' sections.
16. Examples of such ploys can be found in I. V. Good, *The Scientist Speculates*, Heinemann, 1962. Kohn, *op. cit.*, is also useful.
17. J. W. N. Watkins, 'Confession is good for ideas', in D. Edge (ed.), *Experiment*, B.B.C., 1964, pp. 64–70.
18. M. T. Oldcom, 'The ABC's of groupness', *J. Abnormal Sociology*, vol. 5, pp. 6–45, reported in Miner, *op. cit.*
19. Cane and Schroeder, *op. cit.*, pp. 36–45.

Controversy 11. How prejudiced are the British?

1. R. Moore 'Race relations and the rediscovery of sociology', *Brit. J. Soc.*, March 1971, pp. 97–104.
2. Institute of Race Relations, E. J. B. Rose (ed.), *Colour and Citizenship*, Oxford University Press 1969.
3. J. Rex., 'The ethics of research', *New Society*, 7 Aug. 1969, p. 221.
4. Correspondence columns of *New Society*, 14 and 21 Aug., 4 and 11 Sept. 1969.
5. *New Society*, 14 Aug. 1969, p. 262, letter of J. Rowan. *New Society* 21 Aug. 1969, pp. 300–1, letter of D. Lawrence.
6. *New Society*, 4 Sept. 1969, pp. 371–2, letter of M. Abrams.
7. *New Society*, 11 Sept. 1969, p. 408, letters of D. Lawrence and J. Rowan.
8. J. Rex and R. Moore, *Race, Community and Conflict*, Oxford University Press, 1967.

9. J. G. Davies and J. Taylor, 'Race, community and no conflict', *New Society*, 9 July 1970, pp. 67–9.
10. See Davies and Taylor, *op. cit.* Correspondence is in *New Society*, 16, 23 and 30 July 1970.

Chapter 11. The interpretation of results

1. K. R. Popper, *Conjectures and Refutations: Growth of Scientific Knowledge*, Basic Books, 1963.
2. 'Wisconsin studies of the measurement and prediction of teacher effectiveness', *Journal of Experimental Education*, Sept. 1961, pp. 5–156.
3. M. Rutter, B. Maughan, P. Mortimore and J. Ouston, *Fifteen Thousand Hours*, Open Books, 1979.
4. K. Lewin, R. Lippitt and R. K. White, 'Patterns of aggressive behaviour in experimentally created social climates', in E. Amidon and J. Hough, *Interaction Analysis*, Addison-Wesley, 1967, pp. 24–46.
5. R. Lippitt and R. K. White, 'An experimental study of leadership and group life', in H. P. Proshansky and B. Seidenberg, *Basic Studies in Social Psychology*, Holt, Rinehart & Winston, 1965, pp. 523–37.
6. Lewin *et al.*, *op. cit.*, p. 37.
7. J. S. Coleman *et al.*, *Equality of Educational Opportunity*, U.S. Government Printing Office, 1966.
8. C. Jencks *et al.*, *Inequality: A reassessment of the effect of family and schooling in America*, Basic Books, 1972.
9. Rutter *et al.*, *op. cit.*
10. D. Reynolds, D. Jones and S. St. Leger, 'Schools do make a difference', *New Society*, **37**, 1976, p. 321.
11. M. J. Power *et al.*, 'Delinquent Schools', *New Society*, **10**, 1967, pp. 111–32.
12. D. Gath *et al.*, *Child Guidance and Delinquency in a London Borough*, Maudsley Monograph no. 24, Oxford University Press, 1977.
13. Gray and Satterly, *op. cit.* (Controversy 1, n.20).
14. Coleman *et al.*, *op. cit.*
15. H. R. Alker, 'A typology of ecological fallacies', in M. Dogan and S. Rokkan, *Quantitative Ecological Analysis in the Social Sciences*, Massachusetts Institute of Technology Press, 1969.
16. M. W. Riley, *Sociological Research*, Vol. 1, Harcourt, Brace & World, 1963, pp. 700–9.
17. For examples see discussion by D. S. Pugh, 'Organisations: their nature', in F. D. Carver and J. J. Sergiovanni, *Organisations and Human Behaviour*, McGraw-Hill, 1969, pp. 111-29.
18. F. Musgrove and P. H. Taylor, *Society and the Teacher's Role*, Routledge & Kegan Paul, 1969.
19. P. E. Daunt, review of Musgrove and Taylor (above, n.18) in *Universities Quarterly*, Autumn 1969, pp. 479–81.
20. Jordan, *op. cit.* (Contro 5, n.4).
21. D. Riesman, *The Lonely Crowd*, Doubleday, 1953.
22. E. Larrabee, 'David Riesman and his readers', in S. M. Lipset and L. Lowenthal, *Character and Social Structure*, Free Press, 1961.
23. D. Riesman and N. Glazer, 'A reconsideration', in Lipset and Lowenthal, pp. 419–58.

24. J. W. Wiggins and H. Schoeck, 'A profile of the aged: U.S.A.', *Geriatrics*, July 1961, pp. 336–42.
25. L. D. Cain, 'The AMA and the gerontologists: uses and abuses of "A profile of the aged: U.S.A."', in Sjoberg *op. cit.* (ch.3, n.18), pp. 78–114.
26. J. W. Wiggins and H. Schoeck, *Scientism and Values*, Van Nostrand, 1960.

Controversy 12. How formative is infantile experience?

1. J. Bowlby, *Maternal Care and Mental Health*, World Health Organisation, 1951.
2. W. Goldfarb, 'The effects of the early institutional care on adolescent personality', *J. of Exp. Ed.* 12, 1943, pp. 106–29.
3. See P. Morgan, *Child Care. Sense and Fable*, Temple Smith, 1975, pp. 26–7.
4. B. Spock, *Problems of Parents*, Bodley Head, 1963, p. 156.
5. J. Bowlby, *Child Care and the Growth of Love*, Penguin, 1953.
6. R. A. Spitz, 'Hospitalism: an inquiry into the genesis of psychiatric conditions in early childhood', *Psychoanalytic Study of the Child*, 1, 1945, pp. 53–75.
7. B. Wootton, *Social Science and Social Pathology*, Allen & Unwin, 1959.
8. M. Rutter, *Maternal Deprivation Reassessed*, Penguin, 1972.
9. Morgan, *op. cit.*
10. A. M. Clarke and A. D. B. Clarke, *Early Experience: Myth and Evidence*, Open Books, 1976.
11. N. O'Connor, 'The evidence for the permanently disturbing effects of mother-child separation', *Acta Psychologica*, 12, 1956, pp. 174–91.
12. For a valuable critique, see M. Kellmer Pringle's review of the literature in D. Pilling and M. Kellmer Pringle, *Controversial Issues in Child Development*, P. Elek, 1978, pp. 9-20.
13. J. W. D. Douglas, 'Early hospital admissions and later disturbances of behaviour and learning', *Developmental Psychology*, 10, 2, 1975, pp. 255–9.
14. D. Quinton and M. Rutter, 'Early hospital admissions and later disturbances of behaviour: an attempted replication of Douglas's findings', *Dept. of Child and Adolescent Psychiatry, Institute of Psychiatry* (unpublished), 1975.
15. Rutter *et al.*, *op. cit.* (ch.11, n.3).

Chapter 12. The scope and limitations of social research

1. Barker Lunn, *op. cit.* (Controversy 7, n.19).
2. Power *et al.*, *op. cit.* (ch.11, n.11).
3. Rutter *et al.*, *op. cit.* (ch.11, n.3).
4. R. Dubin, 'Theory and research', in T. O'Toole (ed.)), *The Organisation, Management and Tactics of Social Research*, Schenkman, 1971.
5. Inner London Education Authority, *Literacy Survey*, 1974.
6. Hargreaves, *op. cit.* (ch.3, n.23)
7. Rosenthal and Jacobson, *op. cit.* (Controversy 4, n.1).
8. R. Nash, *Classrooms Observed*, Routledge & Kegan Paul, 1973.
9. A. E. Siegel, 'Research on child development', in R. Glaser (ed.), *Research and Development and School Change*, Lawrence Erlbaum, 1978, pp. 47–66.
10. J. W. Getzels, 'Theoretical research and school change', in R. Glaser (ed.), *ibid.*, pp. 27–46.

11. Lewin, Lippitt and White, *op. cit.* (ch.11, n.4).

12. See Controversy 5.

13. E. L. Thorndike and R. S. Woodworth, 'The influence of improvement in one mental function upon the efficiency of other functions', *Psychological Review*, 8, 1901, pp. 247–61, 384–95 and 553–64.

14. E. Charles, 'The effect of present trends in fertility and morality upon the future population of Great Britain and upon its age composition', in L. Hogben, *Political Arithmetic*, Allen & Unwin, 1938, pp.73–105.

15. All figures from Central Statistical Office.

16. Charles, *op. cit.*

17. R. Layard *et al.*, *The Impact of Robbins*, Penguin, 1969.

18. Committee to consider the future numbers of medical practitioners and the appropriate intake of medical students (Willinck Committee), H.M.S.O., 1957.

19. R. H. S. Crossman, *Paying for the Social Services*, Fabian Society, 1969.

20. U.S. Department of Health, Education and Welfare, *The Persistence of Preschool Effects*, October, 1977.

21. Institute of Race Relations, *op. cit.* (Controversy 11, n.2)

22. Barker Lunn, *op. cit.* (Controversy 7, n.19).

23. Ford, *op. cit.* (ch.3, n.17).

24. Barker Lunn, *op. cit.*

25. M. Komoravsky (ed.), *Sociology and Public Policy: The Case of the Presidential Commissions*, Elsevier, 1975.

26. L. Ohlin, 'Report on the President's Commission on Law Enforcement and Administration of Justice', in Komoravsky, *ibid.*, pp. 93–115.

27. M. Kogan, *The Politics of Education*, Penguin, 1971.

INDEX